The Bathtub Murders

Pete Dover

Published by Trellis Publishing, 2021.

While every precaution has been taken in the preparation of this book, the publisher assumes no responsibility for errors or omissions, or for damages resulting from the use of the information contained herein.

THE BATHTUB MURDERS

First edition. July 4, 2021.

Copyright © 2021 Pete Dover.

ISBN: 979-8224699896

Written by Pete Dover.

THE BATHTUB MURDERS

PETE DOVER

Killing Mom – The Story of the Andersen Family

Imagine having kids who can speak five languages by their mid-teens. Daughters who are described by an experienced, senior childcare professional as the most intelligent she has come across in thirty years of working with adolescents.

Can there be a greater dream for loving parents? College awaits, then a top job with all that brings in terms of comfort and lifestyle. Who knows, these caring kids might even look after their mom and dad in old age. But the dream turned into a nightmare for one parent of super-intelligent children.

Linda Anderson's daughters certainly fitted that high IQ category; but unlike other clever kids, they used their intelligence for the most disingenuous of reasons: to plan the murder of their mother. Because, while their intellect might have seen them placed at the top of their class, it bore little influence on their social skills, their moral development or their emotional maturity. The reason for that is something that, if known, remains secretly stored in the files of the Canadian justice system – the probability of mental illness of some kind seems a strong possibility as to the root cause of the kids' decisions. Or, maybe, we will conclude it was pure selfishness that directed their actions.

Linda was a single mom; life was hard. The girls' father had walked out of their lives when the kids were still young. He seemed to play no part in the family now. Not only was the struggling mother trying to bring up Sandra and Beth (the names by which the girls are identified – their real identities remain secret as a result of Canadian law and the fact that, at the time of the crime, they were juveniles). It was not just the two teenage girls for whom she was responsible. There was the girls' brother Bobby as well. To add to Linda's complex existence, she had her own internal demons with which to cope. She suffered from depression.

Back in the late 1990s and early 2000s this debilitating condition was barely understood. The 'shake yourself down and get on with it' school of thought still dominated medical and psychological thinking, and even where doctors were trying to get a handle on the devastating consequences of the mental health disorder they were thwarted by a society that viewed depression as a weakness; something that was evidence of a lack of moral fibre. Depression was, according to the prevailing mood, a tad self-indulgent.

For Linda, one way she coped with her condition was to drink heavily; something that is both a symptom and a cause of depression. However, she retained enough wherewithal to place her kids at the centre of her life – she worked two jobs in an effort to provide for them. At the time of her death, she had just lost one of these. Possibly this may have been a significant factor in the crime soon to take place. The thought that their mom would now be able to give them even less of the material goods Sandra and Beth craved may have been the final straw behind their actions. However, this is something about which we can only speculate.

The Andersens lived in Mississauga, a province of Ontario which is effectively a suburb of Toronto. It is a thriving city with a population of three quarters of a million. Located on the shores of Lake Ontario, and home to the Toronto international airport, it is relatively wealthy, even by Canadian standards. But like all big cities, it also has its impoverished areas. It was in one of these that the Andersens resided.

For all the reasons that could have been behind the Anderson sisters' murder the bottom line is that they enjoyed it. Or so it appeared.

'The excitement, the collaboration, the drama,' observed Dr Phil Klassen, a well-regarded forensic psychiatrist. The good doctor was considering the motivation behind the murder Sandra and Beth committed.

But he overlooked another, very common motive for murder. Greed. No doubt, with an alcoholic mother, times were frequently hard for the girls, but there is nothing to suggest that Linda was anything other than caring, even if she sometimes lacked the wherewithal to demonstrate that love in the way that most parents do.

However, she was also insured, and on her death each girl would inherit $680000. A handy sum when you are fifteen and sixteen. Despite their intelligence, the girls' lack of worldliness shone through when it came to money. Adults know that $68 thousand is a lot of cash – it was worth even more back in 2003 – but it is not enough to live on for life.

Police later discovered that the girls had even planned what they would do with the money. Number one was a big trip to Europe, taking their best friends for company. After all, what more could a couple of mourning teenagers need than the pick me up of a thrilling vacation? Next, they would buy a big, comfortable house for themselves and their brother. No doubt, the pot smoking teens would be holding plenty of parties there; they would become the most popular girls in town...with their peers if not with those friends' parents.

Finally, thinking of the future, they would buy a marijuana farm. Free pot. Brilliant. Quite how the sum for which their mother was insured would provide all of those luxuries they did not consider. All that they thought about was that they would get a lot of money.

In order to deliver their dream, they planned their crime carefully. Quite why they chose their mother as a victim, unless it was just for money, is something to which nobody has ever really gotten to the bottom. Certainly, although she dedicated those days when she was sober to her kids, giving them more than her meagre income supported, they always wanted more. But while the insurance money would provide them with a comfortable existence (if not quite as luxurious as they dreamed) they insisted to friends it was not the main motivation behind their crime. Of course, they may have been lying about this.

Psychiatrists would later stress the selfishness and lack of empathy both girls held. However, there seemed no overwhelming reason to kill their mother, other than frustration with her depression and regular drunkenness. It does not seem as though Linda was abusive towards the girls, at least not from what can be gathered from reports into their lives. At the same time, because the girls were minors, far less details about the case are available to the public than is usual for a murder. As much as anything, it seems as though Linda became their victim because she was the nearest to hand.

It seems as though the girls decided quite early on that they would drown their mother. When police began to realise that Linda's death might not be the result of a tragic but drunken accident, they searched the hard drive of the girls' computer. On it, they discovered more than 14000 hits for a certain keyword – 'drowning'. Close behind were searches for 'codeine' and 'bathtub', or so the media claims.

Their plans were clear: somehow get their mother to consume enough codeine – a chemical present in one of the prescription pills Linda took – to render her helpless. But not enough for it to signal undue alarm in any post-mortem examination. Once she was weakened and compliant, they would drown her in the bathtub.

Like all the best plans, the genius in this lay in its simplicity. Finding the easiest way to achieve a goal is the mark of an intelligent person or, in this case, teenage sisters. Yet, for all the brilliance of their planning and the depth and thoroughness of their research, again they displayed more than a modicum of naivety.

It is a mark of the teenage mind that it does not easily see the consequences of actions. That is why teenagers drive madly, putting not only other road users at risk, but also their own lives. Or they experiment wildly with drugs, without thought to the source of those chemicals they are feeding into their bodies. Simply, they do not consider what might result. Not because they do not want to, but because the frontal cortex of their brain is undeveloped, and that is what helps to identify risk. Since they fail to see risk in what they do, so they do little or nothing to mitigate it.

And it is this lack of consideration towards consequences that the Andersen girls now display. Because having planned their attack so thoroughly, they share the details of their intentions with friends. They do not consider that what friends might find a laugh when they are fifteen might later play on their conscience. Or, a person who is buddy with whom you can trust your closest secret today could turn into an enemy over the course of a couple of unstable months.

However, for now these friends demonstrated the twisted, misguided loyalty of teenage bonding and kept the girls' secret to themselves. Shortly, we shall consider in more detail the reasoning behind the indefensible decisions of some of these teens. Although, to be fair, it is the nature of young adolescents to boast, and much of what is claimed, especially online, is no more than a fantasy dreamworld never to be enacted in real life.

Still, on this occasion, the crime went ahead. The girls made a cocktail of vodka and codeine for their mother who, no doubt grateful that her daughters were doing something for her, drank it down as planned. Again, this was no spur of the moment decision, but a carefully planned process. The girls began the task of getting their mother drunk around lunchtime, and it was a scheme that took several hours to advance.

Soon, though, Linda was partially sedated, the codeine slowing her heartbeat, her reactions and her sense of what was going on. What happened next is a mark of the callousness of the teenage girls. Even while their biological mother, the woman who brought them into world, who nurtured them and helped them through the trials and tribulations of growing up, lay partially conscious, the drugs doing their deadly work inside of her, they boasted of their actions online to friends.

'Good luck – wear gloves,' replied one.

They ran a warm bath for their mother and helped her into it. They offered to give her a relaxing massage, before telling her to turn onto her stomach so that they could concentrate on her back. Then, following the probably unnecessary advice of the heartless friend, Sandra, the older sister, donned a pair of latex gloves. She pushed her mother below the surface and lacking the strength to fight off the water entering her lungs, the 43-year-old mother, victim of depression and alcoholism, felt life drift away. Sandra held her there, below the surface, until her mother was dead.

Even then, there seems to have been neither remorse nor sorrow for their actions. Instead, the girls went out to meet friends, establishing their alibi should it be needed. The alibi included celebrating their success in a restaurant. But, to be fair, who really suspects a pair of teenage girls of murdering their mother? Disbelief was probably the best alibi of all.

With their friends, the girls bragged about the experience they, but none of the others present, had been through. 'It was not as hard as we thought,' boasted Sandra.

Now the plan must enter its final stages. When the girls return home, they 'discover' the body of their mother lying face down in the bath. It is time for some acting. Distraught, they ring the emergency services. The operator instructs them how to give CPR, but they are too upset to comply. With great, gulping gasps of distress they await the arrival of the paramedics. When these people reach the house, they are confronted by two inconsolable girls and the body of their dead mother.

The girls are treated with sympathy by all. They have, it seems, succeeded in their aim and gotten away with their crime.

Their success soon goes to their heads. Not only does Sandra embroider stories of her callous derring-do to her close friends, but she shares details with everybody she meets at parties. It is stupidity of the highest order. She feels untouchable; unchallengeable, top dog. She is proud, arrogant, over-confident. In fact, the only emotion that seems not to break the unpleasant surface of her consciousness is remorse.

Even that statement is too simplistic for these complex personalities. Pity, too, stays hidden. As do sadness and guilt. In fact, the soft emotions which define most people appeared to be lacking in her and, it has to be said, her sister's make up.

But the stupidity came home to roost. Inevitably, stories began to spread; the cracks in the sisters' front began to appear and judgement day began to close in. The only surprise, given the naïve and loose tongued behaviour of the girls, is that it took a year to come to light. But emerge the story did. From what shaky evidence exists, it would appear as though Sandra was the one who gave away the game. The police persuaded a friend (of sorts) to have a wire placed in his car and soon Sandra was damned by her own lips as she revealed, once more, the gruesome details of the crime of which she was so proud. Beth, too, was caught describing her part in the matricide.

That the person who eventually went to the police was a man perhaps gives a little insight into another side of Sandra. Her insecurity. She was much taken by this man when she met him and wanted to impress. Her way to do this was to boast, to a virtual stranger, of the murder of her mother. It is of little surprise that he took his concerns to the authorities – it seems remarkable that such an action took so long in coming given the number of people with whom Sandra, and to a lesser extent Beth, spilt their secret.

Perhaps, in defense of a public who seemed unable or unwilling to follow a course of action most of us would feel we would take – that is taking the tale to the authorities, we have to believe that the people to whom the story was told simply did not believe it was true.

Bob Mitchell, a reporter with the Toronto Star, makes even that view hard to believe. He interviewed a number of the friends of Linda and Beth. His report hid their real identities, but nevertheless their stories are compelling.

'Ashley' was close to Sandra and had tried, half-heartedly, to prevent her from carrying out the crime she had planned. The murder occurred on January 18th, 2003, and in the days following she agonised over what else she could have done to stop it from taking place.

Not through sympathy for the victim – Ashley held no fondness for Linda Andersen. But because the entire event made her feel uncomfortable. 'It was so creepy,' she told Mitchell. 'There really won't be any Linda Andersen around anymore,' That thought was what had hit her when she had taken a ghoulish trip to the funeral parlour where Linda's body was lying in an open casket.

Later, she reflected on the inaction of herself and her friends. 'We're all smart kids. We knew what was going on. We weren't helpless teenagers. All of us could have picked up a phone. The fact is, we didn't.'

Another friend, reported under the pseudonym 'Jay', had been told about the Andersen girls' plans before Christmas in 2002. He had begun to date Beth, although it was Sandra who shared more of the details. At one stage, he had even planned to help them to provide an alibi, by going to Jack Astor's for dinner with them. But common sense prevailed, and he withdrew from involvement in the crime. He too, in his heart, believed that it was all talk. A childish game that would never take physical form. He remembers his shock when, the day after the murder, he learned the truth.

Jay was one of the few people to report any kind of regret in the behaviour of the sisters. He told how Sandra had been tearful and remorseful when they had bumped into each other in a shopping mall a few days after the event. She had told him how she watched her mother's skin physically change colour in front of her as the life drained from her body. She also told how Beth had stood by, watching, seemingly transfixed by what was taking place.

Jay also told Bob Mitchell of his fears. When the police finally began investigating the crime, he was sure he would be dragged in as an accomplice, charged because he had made suggestions to the girls, including advice to wear gloves.

The whole escapade proved to be a life lesson to Jay. He learned that keeping the secret of what happened was wrong. That he should have spoken to someone; ideally the police, but even his parents if he could not bring himself to go to the authorities. But he had not, and he knew that his refusal to betray his friends was, in truth, an act of cowardice. It was a pity that the lesson he learned came at such a cost.

Donny was another friend. His reason for not going to the police was that he thought he was madly in love with Sandra. In fact, he had not been in on the plans of the crime. He developed his own suspicions when Sandra phoned him the next day.

'My mother died last night. She drowned in the bathtub,' she reported.

Later, he realised how ludicrous that sounded, like something out of a 1920s silent comedy. They spoke again a few hours on, and he started to become suspicious.

'Where was Bobby?' he had asked, referring to the girls' younger brother. The answer – 'He was over at his father's.' – seemed too convenient.

The girls went to stay at their Aunt Martha's house. (According to the far from factually accurate 'Perfect Sisters' film, based on the lives of Andersens, the aunt was their pillar of strength in the aftermath of Linda's death. Until, that is, she learned the truth, when she abandoned the girls like a pair of rabid dogs, leaving them to their fate.) Donny met them there and began to ask about the dinner they claimed to be at when their mother died. Specifically, he was wondering why he had not been invited.

By the following week his suspicions were sufficiently raised for the alarm bells to sound in Sandra. She decided it was time to tell him the truth.

'What would you do if you knew I had killed someone?' she asked him.

Over the next few days gradually the story came out. 'What went through your mind when you did it?' asked Donny with a mixture of macabre interest and genuine disbelief. Sandra's answer gave further insight into her mixed-up mental state. She killed her mother to stop her becoming a vegetable, she said. 'Some lives need to be taken,' she told him.

Another who became embroiled in the case was the boyfriend of one of the girls. Once more, in order to protect the identity of minors, the man's name was not made public. However, a chat log was discovered by police which brought the young felon to justice. 'Your mom gets Tylenol 3's, right?' he asked his girlfriend.

With the lack of awareness of a self-centred teen, she replied 'Probably.'

'Seriously, you should include them in the game plan,' he continued. 'I'm not talking 20 here. I mean like five.'

(When Linda was found later, the codeine discovered in her blood indicated that she had consumed between four and six if the Tylenol 3 pills.)

The boyfriend went on to write: 'I'm involved this much, I'm willing to help you out with any of it.' Which he did. He suggested the girls buy a movie ticket for a show running through the time they killed their mother, providing them with an alibi as to their location. The paper trail, said the boyfriend, would confuse the police and any suspicion falling on the girls would quickly disappear. The man later told the court that his suggestions were not meant seriously. Instead, they were just a fantasy game of the kind kids play. The fact that the girls did not take up his suggestion may have counted in his favour.

The role of the boyfriend offers interest beyond the murder itself. When his appeal reached the Supreme Court of Canada, that body was forced to define the stage at which a person becomes a part of a conspiracy to commit a crime.

A lower court had found the man guilty of conspiracy to commit murder, and he had received an eighteen-month sentence. However, while the appeal court upheld his conviction, it reduced his sentence to eight months behind bars with a further four months under supervision.

The question of what constitutes being a part of a conspiracy was one which Canadian law had failed to answer conclusively up to that point. Indeed, it depended on the part of the country in which a defendant was tried as to the definition that would be used. For example, in British Colombia and, relevantly for this case, Ontario a wide view was taken. A person who knowingly committed an act – even just a verbal contribution - which made it easier for others to commit a crime could be judged a part of a conspiracy. Other provinces, though, took a narrower view. In Quebec and Alberta, for example, to be included in a conspiracy a person had to directly aid or abet an agreement to commit a crime. A much harder definition to prove.

In reaching their decision, the Supreme Court decided to err more on the side of provinces like Quebec and Alberta. The judges did, however, have a final warning for the man. Although his sentence was dramatically reduced, Justice Michael Moldaver (presenting the view of the court) told him that his contribution could have been judged to have played a part in committing a first-degree murder, which would have carried a far heavier sentence.

The girls were arrested just over a year after their crime, on January 21st, 2004. When it came to their trial, a guilty verdict for first degree murder was quickly imposed on both. Canadian laws with regards to crimes committed by children are more liberal than in many countries. The authorities take the view that young minds can change, that rehabilitation is possible. It is a forward-thinking outlook. Whether it was right for Sandra and Beth is harder to determine. Certainly, psychologists shared their doubts over the suitability of release, for Sandra in particular, when the time came. Reports indicate that Sandra remained unable to empathise with others, and still seemed to feel no remorse for her actions. She was still self-centred and completely egotistical, to an extent which probably placed her into a mentally ill category. Whatever, the authorities decided that it was time for the girls to return to society, and to put their lives back on track.

In the event, the girls served just under half of their sentence behind bars, including the time spent in custody before their trial. Because of Canadian law, their identities will remain a secret forever. After their release to a halfway house, both sought to further their education. Sandra, for example, earned a $2000 scholarship to study at the University of Waterloo.

The release of 'The Perfect Sisters' in 2014 seemed to be the final act in the circus. The movie starred Mira Sorvino as Linda plus Abigail Breslin and Georgie Henley as the murderous daughters who took her life. It followed the publication of 'The Class Project: How to Kill a Mother: The True Story of Canada's Infamous Bathtub Girls', a book by the aforementioned Toronto journalist Bob Mitchell, which covered the story in forensic detail.

Both the book and the film have been criticised in some quarters for glorifying the crime, and perhaps presenting the girls in a light more favourable than their action deserves. That, of course, depends to a large extent on the viewpoint we hold regarding their crime.

The adolescent mind is a complex organ; especially so when perhaps unstable, as it may have been in Sandra's case, and under the heavy influence of another as seems likely with Beth. In most cases, it can, and does, change as adulthood arrives. Then again, matricide is a (fortunately) rare enough crime, one made even more unusual when the perpetrators boast about their actions.

But let us hope that the Canadian authorities were right to grant lifetime anonymity to whoever are the real people behind Beth and Sandra Andersen; that little Bobby, who seemed to disappear quickly from the story, has recovered as much as possible from the tragedy; and that rehabilitation is complete. And successful.

THE MURDER OF ROSEANN QUINN

PETER DOVER

When does an enjoyment of varied interests become a double life? That is a question pertinent to the tragic and strange tale of Roseann Quinn. Many will be familiar with this name, even though her death dates back three and a half decades. That is because the case of Roseann Quinn is the one behind the well known 1977 film, 'Looking for Mr Goodbar', which starred Diane Keaton.

It is also the inspiration for Judith Rossner's slightly less well known but still best selling novel of the same name, and the account by the New York Times journalist, Lacey Fosburgh (called 'Closing Time: The True Story of the Goodbar Murder.')

Sometimes, it can be tricky to understand why some crimes make their way to the eye of popular culture and other, equally tragic, events fail to do so. Although, of course, every death is a tragedy for someone. But in the case of Roseann, the answer is clear to see.

Let us spend a moment or two considering what career we might hold up as the epitome of good work, of social benefit. Doctor, nurse, nun? To that list most would add elementary school teacher. But when that educator of the youngest members of our society seeks to specialise in working with the disabled, the neediest of all, then they come closer to sainthood. Roseann was an elementary school teacher, and was developing a specialisation in working with deaf children when she met her untimely death. All of that is enough to warrant a special place for her in the minds of the nation, but take that perfection and flavour it with a taste of a double life, an aspect of living that we would not associate with such a vocation, and our interest is firmly aroused.

Were she alive today, Roseann would have entered deserved retirement from her career. She was born just prior to the end of the Second World War, in 1944. John and her mother, also Roseann, were strongly catholic Irish Americans. The young teacher to be was born in the Bronx, in an aspirational middle class family.

She had three siblings – her two brothers John (the parents liked to pass on the family names) and Dennis. She also had a sister called

Donna. Aged just eleven, Roseann and her family moved out of the Bronx to the rapidly expanding small New Jersey Township of Mine Hill. This was a comfortably middle class, mostly white, Republican small town and perfectly suited the kind of family of which 1950s America boasted. One could almost feel the post war boom in such a community, and the Quinn's (despite their Irish heritage and its associated stereotypes) typified that. John was an executive with the large, nearby organisation Bell Laboratories. All was bright, all was rosy.

The first small blip on the horizon came when Roseann was just thirteen. She developed a condition called scoliosis. With this illness the spine grows in an S shape. It typically affects children as they head through the growth spurts of puberty and is only dangerous in the most serious of cases, where the growth can put pressure on the lungs, resulting in breathing problems. However, in Roseann's case the condition was bad enough to see her spend a year in hospital. But she recovered and headed on to the Morris Catholic High School in Denville, New Jersey.

Her year out did not impact educationally on the quiet, well liked and friendly girl. She graduated successfully and entered teacher training college at the Newark State Teachers College.

The picture is emerging of a young woman who appeared as the opposite of the drug taking, high living, sex fuelled state of twenty somethings we like to picture as symbolic of the 1960s. Following her graduation, this image became even shinier. She gained three years standard teaching experience and then moved into a school for the deaf, working with a class of eight year olds.

She was a popular young teacher, adored by parents and students alike, and respected by her more senior colleagues. Her time was dedicated to her class; she would often stay behind after school supporting them. 'The students loved her,' said a spokesman for her school when news of her death became public. During this time she decided that she wanted to understand more about working with the deaf, and entered into a part time post graduate course.

Slim, attractive and bookish, with large tinted glasses, Roseanne moved into a recently converted apartment in New York. It might not be in the swankiest of homes, but was not a bad way of living for a young, single and poorly paid professional. There she enjoyed a cosmopolitan life. She was the kind of woman who fell easily into company. She had a wide circle of friends, and not just from the world of education. The early part of the 1970s saw the women's movement growing fast. The sexual revolution was underway. If Roseann Quinn bought into this, and it seemed as though she did, then it was in a bookish way. Her carefully decorated West Side studio apartment was not necessarily what might be a typical teacher's home. Nor would this profession be known for sitting alone in bars, drinking wine and reading.

More typical, perhaps, was her diverse circle of friends – artists, professionals, construction workers from all racial groups - she was a true liberal in her attitudes.

It is now that we begin to consider the allegations of a double life which came to prominence following her murder. Perhaps 'double life' is too strong a term. We are in the 1970s, the emancipation of women is speeding up, for a woman steeped in the strongly conservative values of a deeply catholic background, cosmopolitan West side New York must have been like stepping into a kaleidoscope of colour and opportunity.

Yes, Roseann was dedicated, intellectual, sincere. But she was also friendly and, put bluntly, enjoyed the company of the opposite sex. To be single, attractive, in your late twenties and taking full, liberal advantage of that might not have been atypical of her background, but things change. And why not?

It was easy to see why Roseann had not settled down. There were two reasons; her career and her simple enjoyment of a variety of men. A double life? Well, maybe. But that term comes with connotations which are undeserved for a woman who gave so much to her community.

If there is to be a criticism of Roseann Quinn, it is simply that her judgement in choosing the men she led back to the small apartment was not always the best. Perhaps she was attracted to a certain kind of man, perhaps it was simply that this kind of man saw a vulnerability and availability in her. Whichever, neighbours often reported sounds of raised voices and fighting from her apartment. On one occasion, she emerged the next day with a scratched face and a black eye.

Then, on New Year's Day, 1973, tragedy occurred. Roseann followed her regular pattern for when she was not working. In the early evening, she set off by herself to a bar, W M Tweeds, just opposite her home. There, she met with two men – Danny Murray who was a stock broker and his gay lover John Wayne Wilson. The two had been an item for around a year.

To join up with a couple of gay men, back in a time when such behaviour was still frowned upon, was typical of Roseann's liberalism. Indeed, even though the Stonewall riots of a few years back had brought homosexuality into the open, same sex sexual relationships were still, at that time in New York, technically illegal.

When Murray left the bar an hour short of midnight, Roseann and Wilson continued to drink. They decided to head back to her apartment. It was the last time she was seen alive in public.

Three days later her school sent round a teacher to check on their normally highly committed and professional employee. It was completely out of character for her to be absent without informing her employers. Letting down her class and her colleagues was not something with which she was in any way associated. The teacher found the caretaker, and together they went to investigate.

Roseann was dead, murdered and mutilated in horrific fashion. She had been raped and stabbed at least 14 times. She had been beaten on the head using an ornamental metal bust of herself. Bizarrely, a candle had been inserted into her vagina. The apartment was ransacked, and blood spattered the walls. It appeared as though she had been killed in a frenzy of violence.

Police began searching for the last people to see her, and soon identified Murray and Wilson as suspects. But the latter of the two was nowhere to be found. However, Murray quickly admitted that Wilson had confessed the crime to him. He had given his partner cash to travel to his home state of Indiana, where he could stay with his brother.

Within a few days Wilson was arrested and stories of his past began to surface. They were complex to say the least. Wilson was just twenty three years old at the time of his arrest, but in that short life he had married, divorced and fathered two daughters. He had moved from Indiana to Florida, and then on to New York.

Wilson also had a police record, but not one that suggested the kind of violence that had been enacted on Roseann. He had been arrested in Florida on charges of disorder, and served a short spell in prison in Daytona. Then, he had spent time in jail in Kansas on charges of larceny.

In fact, but the time he had hooked up with Murray, he was an escapee from a third prison, this time one in Miami. He had made his way to New York and worked as a street hustler, before joining up with Murray and beginning their sexual partnership. Quite a lot to have achieved by your early twenties.

However, despite his time in prison Wilson was not a hardened criminal; he soon confessed to police his crime, and the murder may well have fallen into the files of the many hideous events that are too numerous to stay in the public's consciousness for long. That was not to be.

Wilson informed the police that he and Roseann were drunk when they arrived back at the fashionable West side apartment. They had moved onto pot: more evidence of Roseann's double life or just the expected behaviour of a single twenty something in the early 70s?

They had fallen into bed – Roseann was eventually discovered on the sofa bed in the apartment's only room – but Wilson had been unable to maintain an erection. He claimed to police that Roseann had taunted him at this point, criticising his sexual performance and mocking his manhood. He had, in the drug and alcohol induced state, suffered a huge and unexpected surge of anger, and had killed his victim in a moment of lost control.

An open and shut case. Or so it should have been, but for another episode which personifies life in the early 1970s. Some would argue it holds true even today. Firstly, once in prison Wilson fell into depression. He was sent for an analysis of his mental and emotional state, which the defence planned to use in mitigation of his crimes. But such considerations were in their infancy back then. Mental health was a cause of amusement and mockery rather than sympathy and understanding. The hospital was small, the psychologists over stretched and underfunded and the priority awarded to a murderer was low in the extreme. Wilson's diagnosis was delayed, then delayed again. In fact, he never reached the stage of seeing a person who may have helped him through his emotional crisis.

Perhaps the State felt that such time and attention was unwarranted. Technically, in 1973 New Jersey still employed the death penalty although in practice nobody had been executed since Ralph Hudson ten years previously. He had been sent to the electric chair after beating his wife to death while on Christmas leave from another sentence he was serving.

Yet there can be little doubt that Wilson was suffering from depression. He was placed on suicide watch, but just as was the case with his psychological analysis, there was a difference between appointment and practice. His New York jail had only a small number of cells in their designated 'suicide watch' section; they were full. There was a long waiting list for them.

So Wilson remained in the main body of the prison. When, one night four months after his arrest, he complained to a guard of his low mood and wish to commit suicide, the guard responded with expected understanding and sympathy.

He offered to supply Wilson with extra sheets so he could use them to hang himself. Indeed, he went further, actually providing the sheets of which Wilson took advantage. Wilson took his own life, and the case was effectively closed.

But that was not the end. However much our modern understanding of the ravaging impacts of mental illness might persuade us towards some sympathy for Wilson, we can still recognise that he was the murderer and Roseann was the victim. It was not the other way round.

That was not how the police appeared to see things, though. Perhaps they were unduly influenced by the tabloid press of the day. And that august body might defend itself by saying it simply reflected the views of the majority of citizens.

The night edition of the New York Daily news for January 5th 1973, a couple of days after Roseann's murder, ran the sensationalist but not hugely controversial headline 'Teacher Victim of Sex Slaying; Battered with Statue of Self'. The juxta position of 'teacher' and 'sex' might raise an eyebrow but otherwise the heading was no more than would be expected from a journal of its kind.

By the time of the final edition, though, the story had taken on a much more lurid twist. 'Teacher Found Nude and Slain' ran the new headline. She was a teacher, and she was nude. Teacher's don't do nude; they wear their underwear in the bath (actually, swimwear, even underwear and pedagogy were incongruous to 1970s America). But if she was a teacher and nude, so the question was raised (in all right thinking people of that enlightened era): didn't she deserve – in part at least – all that she got? The 'Me Too' campaign was still decades away.

But not everybody shared that opinion. Modern women, in particular, refused to see their kind as victims who contributed to their own demise. Over the coming years that viewpoint gained an ever stronger foothold. So the murder and rape of Roseann Quinn became an essential part of the history of the exploitation of women. Exploitation in New York city – in the US as a whole. Indeed, in the entire Western world. Because, in 1973, the rape and murder of a woman is only properly newsworthy if that victim is especially young or especially old – the public can demonstrate suitable outrage at such a crime. Or if she is suitably rich or famous – we all love to read about celebrity. Or, if she is remarkably beautiful.

In a November issue of Time Magazine just a couple of months before Roseann's murder, a former New York City Deputy Police Commissioner had written with disturbing honesty about the police's reaction to serious crime. Robert Daley was speaking before the days when PR experts and political correctness would hide the true values of our major institutions, perhaps making them even more dangerous because of any lack of transparency.

'In New York last year,' he wrote 'we had 1466 murders and many attempted murders. We in the police hierarchy took a personal interest in a few of these: the murder of cops, the Joe Colombo (a contemporary gangster) hit and one or two rape murders distinguished by the youth and beauty of the victim.'

Since we know that rapists consider the beauty of their victims pretty low down their criteria for committing their crime, that the police hierarchy should consider it as paramount is extremely worrying. Or, as might be the case in 1973, extremely normal.

The rape of a beautiful woman sold papers. It sold more if it could be turned into the sort of fantasy certain men might enjoy. And if it became important in the press, so it became important to the police. A very vicious (partly understandable but never justifiable) circle.

And so the murder of Roseann Quinn moved from the merely tragic for her friends and family to one of social importance within the depiction of women by the press, the treatment of women from the police, and the regard of women by (many) men.

If Roseann was found nude, then, goes the thinking, she was egging on her man. If, as Wilson claims, she mocked him for his impotence, then she was entering territory where, well, it is ground from where women are best to stay away. The bedroom is not a banter filled man's locker room but the place where the real business occurs. A man deserves a certain respect. Lead him on, then ridicule him, and frankly (according to the tone sent out by the police over the subsequent months) women deserve what they get.

We might like to think that such misogyny is a thing of the past. But the revelations to emerge from the 'Me Too' campaign suggest that it may not be.

That is perhaps why Roseann's story endures so well today. Yes, being made into a film (or, at least, being the inspiration for one) helps, but does not fully explain why today blogs and articles, TV documentaries and even a rock opera have continued to keep this twenty eight year old teacher's name alive.

Her story illuminates a state of man. Or Woman. Probably both. It could be transferred to Chicago or, with shorts and t shirts replacing the jersey and slacks, to Los Angeles. It could – and does – emerge in London and Paris, Buenos Aires and Tokyo, Shanghai and Lisbon. Hers is the story of individuality subsumed by the machine of social mores. Remember, Roseann is a normal girl. There is little about her that is extra-ordinary when she is viewed from afar. Even the second most abnormal element of her life – behind being murdered – is, in some ways, a sign of her ordinariness. Being hospitalised for a year is unusual, but doesn't everyone have something unusual in their upbringing? It is the absence of abnormality in life that is abnormal.

Of course, when we get into the real person, we see her uniqueness. But the media is not interested in fine detail, it prefers broad brush strokes of vivid, lurid colour. So the 'double life' is created. Teacher versus loner. Worker with the disabled versus sex addict. Or, as we might more properly say, a woman enjoying the new found freedoms of her time.

She heads to the city and makes a life. The life ends in violence and sex, a sordid death with a head bashed in and a vagina stuffed with a candle. It is why, says everybody who celebrates their uniformity, we shouldn't go to the city. Why we shouldn't have one night stands with strangers. Why we should not be alone.

If this were just a story for the 1970s, it would matter less, but it is not.

Leonard Freed, the New York photographer who caught the mood of the seventies better than most, describes an event whereby a young girl stops police to tell them that she has been raped by friends of her boyfriend. He has looked on, and not intervened. As she tells her story, neighbours scream abuse. To speak to the police in that neighbourhood is worse than to be raped. She deserves what she got.

Perhaps the greatest irony of all is that the Goodbar stories take the horror of what happened to Quinn, but then ensure that her life is exaggerated to the extent that sympathy we might hold for a normal woman of her age and time is stretched into voyeurism. The film meant to remember a victim exploits her as much as Wilson, the media, the police.

Her teaching is used merely as a counter balance to her numerous sexual encounters. Not, as in Roseann's real life, as a fundamental (perhaps the most fundamental) part of it. Her sex life is so active that, if true, the real Roseann would have had no time for her further studies, no time to prepare the lessons that made her into the 'much loved' teacher she actually was; certainly no energy to see her through the long, hard days of being a teacher of young deaf children, especially one who commits herself to the well being of her charges well beyond the span of the bells marking the start and end of her days.

But then, if it were to reflect the truth, who would go to see the film? Even when it stars Diane Keaton? Even if she frequently appears in the nude? (A condition allowed in actresses but not in teachers, it would seem). Certainly the audience for such a film would more likely consist of the donnish sociology types than those after either social or sexual titillation. And there are less of the intellectuals. Fewer bums on seats. Smaller takings at the box office. Such a film would not, either, be likely to draw an actor with the pulling power of Richard Gere.

So a tragic death in horrific circumstances is used as the starting point for a film fundamentally about a sexy teacher (and who doesn't like one of those? No doubt Freud could pin point some biological need satisfied by the provision of school milk by our kindergarten mistresses). In its way, a piece of cinema alleging to be a celebration of a life and the eulogy to a death are as exploitative as the men who beat and, eventually, kill the Roseanns, and the hundreds like her across the city, the country, the world.

Incidentally, in Rossner's novel (and the subsequent film) the eponymous Goodbar is the (unsubtle) name of the bar which, in real life, was W M Tweedy.

We cannot escape the unwitting role Roseann has played in the development of the rights of women over the last forty five years. Maybe, she looks down proudly, if a little sadly for all she has had to abandon in becoming the poster girl for women's rights. The feminist writer Susan Brownmiller analysed how victims of rape are presented in the tabloid press. If they are beautiful, then it is in a way that allows men to fantasise over their victimhood. If they are not, then they are hardly reported, unless some other sensationalist idea can be developed to sell the story.

The message is worrying on many levels. It suggests that all men are prone to violence and sexual aggression. Hopefully, only the minority of narrow thinkers would support that notion today, but the rise of internet pornography, the continued stories of sexual exploitation suggest that, if not the norm, then the condition is at least wide spread.

In his Nobel Prize winning novel 'Lord of the Flies' the author William Golding writes about the 'darkness of man's heart.' It is a powerful line; Golding could be referring to man in the widest sense of human life, or simply the male species. It is difficult to be sure. The book itself has no female characters. Even the protagonist, Ralph, speaks more about his Father (capital deliberate) than his mother (lower case equally deliberate). The only female to merit any attention is Piggy's overpowering Aunt. As the name suggest, Piggy becomes a victim in the dystopian story. The novel is devoid of sex – it was written in the 1950s and features twelve year old boys from (Piggy apart) England's most prestigious schools, so any notion of sex is properly avoided – but is full of violence. The message Golding conveys is clear. Despite any advantages we might have in life, our overriding motivation is violence. For adults, we may add the words 'and sex'.

At least, that is the message to which the tabloid press has played. And, the police to whom the attractiveness of a victim determines the attention given to the crime. Also to the film industry, for whom sensationalism always out paces reality.

Maybe times are changing. Maybe not. Sexual predators still exist. Broad stroke views of what is acceptable and what is not might be different, but are still as simplistic. The implication in 1973 might have been that Roseann Quinn got what she deserved because she was a teacher who liked to have sex with men. That would probably hold little weight today. But try suggesting the opposite. Post on social media a view that is not in the increasingly narrow list of what is politically right on, such as that a person might, for whatever reason, make a false accusation and ruin a man (or woman's) life. Do so and the full weight of Facebook will descend upon your head. You will be blocked as readily as Roseann was blamed.

However, for all the associations of her case, it is with Roseann Quinn that we should end. In a way she was a victim who became a cause. A just cause, but one nevertheless. If a person comes to inspire a crusade then their own personal characteristics are easily lost. They become washed in the tide of progress. And lost in it. We should never forget that, more than anything else, Roseann Quinn was a great teacher.

And an undeserving victim

THE BEAUMONT CHILDREN

BARBARA DUKE

It was a warm summer morning on January 26, 1966, when the three Beaumont children left their suburban home to celebrate Australia Day at the beach. The children regularly made the trip by themselves, so their mother felt at ease providing them with bus fare and sending them on their way while she visited and had lunch with a close friend. However, she would return home that afternoon to find that the children still had not returned. That morning would end up being the last time she saw her three children.

Jane (aged 9), Arnna (aged 7), and Grant (aged 4), lived in Somerton Park, a quiet suburb minutes away from Adelaide, South Australia. Their father, Jim Beaumont, was a linen goods salesman who frequently traveled for work and their mother, Nancy Beaumont, was a stay-at-home mother.

The oldest child, Jane, was viewed by her parents as responsible enough to supervise the other children for short trips and adventures, a style of parenting that was the norm in Australia at that time. The children frequently took the five-minute bus ride to neighboring Glenely Beach by themselves and were looking forward to celebrating the national holiday at the beach.

The children left their home at 10:00am that morning and were seen arriving at the beach by witnesses at 10:15am. They spent much of that morning at play on the beach and were supposed to arrive home at 2:00pm. When they did not arrive at the appointed time, their mother assumed that they had become preoccupied with celebrating the holiday with their playmates and that they would arrive on the next bus or had decided to walk home, something that the three children had done before. When the children did not disembark from the next scheduled bus, their mother began to grow worried.

The disappearance of the Beaumont children would result in one of the largest manhunts and police investigations in Australian history. Furthermore, the event had widespread consequences on Australian society, shattering the illusion that many parents had regarding their children's safety and changing the way that Australians parented their children forever.

Timeline of Events

10:00am - The children leave their Somerton Park home to travel to Glenely Beach by bus.

10:15am - They are seen exiting the bus by multiple witnesses.

11:00am - The three children are spotted playing beneath a sprinkler by an elderly woman. A tall blond man is spotted lying on the ground next to them, watching the children play.

11:15am - A tall blond man is seen playing with the children. They all appear to be laughing and at ease.

11:45am - The children purchase several pastries and a meat pie from the beach snack shop.

12:15pm - The tall blond man and the children are seen leaving the beach together. The children are witnessed laughing together and holding hands.

3:00pm - A postman on his route spots the children walking along Jetty Road alone, away from the beach. The postman is known to the children and they exchange greetings. Police believe that the timeline for this event is incorrect.

7:20pm - The parents of the children become gravely concerned and file a missing children's report with the local police department. Jim Beaumont and the local police search the entire Glenely Beach area.

8:40pm - Police search the surrounding beaches with no results. The father contacts friends and relatives in an attempt to locate the children.

10:00pm - Police issue public radio announcements with a missing children report.

Points of Interest

There are several details in this story which raised doubts with both the parents of the children and the local police department. When the children departed for Glenely Beach in the morning of January 26th, they left with only enough money to cover their bus fare: six shilling and a sixpence. However, the shop owner, who sold several pastries and a meat pie to the children at 11:45am, reported that the children paid for the food with a $1 bill, an amount of money that they did not have when they left their mother's care.

In addition, the shop owner knew the children well and had sold them food and pastries several times before. He reported that the children had never purchased a meat pie before. This suggests that the children received the money from someone after leaving their parents home and that they may have been purchasing the meat pie for someone else.

Lastly, the mother of the children, Nancy Beaumont, repeatedly said that her children were quite shy and very unlikely to speak with strangers, indicating that they may have met the tall blond man prior to the date of their disappearance. Their mother also remembered a seemingly innocuous comment from Arnna, who had previously told her mother that Jane had "got a boyfriend down the beach." Nancy assumed that her daughter was referring to a young playmate, but in hindsight it seems that she may have been referring to the tall blond man spotted by witnesses.

Police Investigation

The South Australian police force began investigating the disappearance of the children in full-force the evening of their disappearance. After interviewing several witnesses who were present at Glenely Beach, they were able to determine that the children were playing with a tall blond, "thin-faced" man while at the beach. He was described as being a blond man in his late 30s with a thin or athletic build.

"Things seemed bungled from the get-go," forensic psychologist Paula Orange said. "First off, the artist drawing the picture admitted to being drunk at the time of completing his task. So the sketch made of the suspect looks more like a lantern-jawed alien than a real person. Secondly, the witnesses claimed that the man was in his late thirties. Witnesses are notorious for getting ages wrong and the police dismissed too many possible subjects out of hand because they didn't fit the profile."

Several witnesses stated that the man was seen dressing the children prior to leaving the beach. The children's parents said that the kids, especially Jane, were very shy and unlikely to speak to a stranger. This later led police to theorize that the children had met the man in question prior to the date of their disappearance and had grown to know him over a period of several weeks.

The blond man and three children were seen leaving the beach together at 12:15pm, after the children purchased several pastries and a meat pie from a local vendor with a $1 bill, an amount of money that they did not have when they left their home that morning.

A wrench was thrown into the investigation when a postman, who knew the children and was on friendly terms with them, reported that he saw the children around 3:00pm that afternoon walking away from the beach and in the direction of their home in Somerton Park. He stated that he exchanged greetings with the young children and that they seemed to be in good spirits. In particular, the postman said that he say the children were "holding hands and laughing" as they walked down the road alone, with no blond companion in sight. Police later said that they believed the postman was mistaken about the timeline and that he most likely saw the children walking some time before noon.

Several months later, a woman in a nearby neighborhood contacted police and told them that she had seen a man with two girls and a young boy enter an abandoned house on her street. She also reported seeing the young boy walking away from the house before he was roughly grabbed by, and returned to the house with, the older man. She never saw the man or children again.

"The response from the public was overwhelming," Orange said. "People drove from miles away to aid in the search. They combed the beach and drained part of it all to no avail. They found nothing, not a trace."

The police were quickly able to eliminate drowning as the cause of the children's disappearance as a result of several witnesses saying that they saw the children leave the beach around 12:15pm. Furthermore, all of the children's belongings were missing, lending further support to the theory that they left the beach. After speaking with the parents, the police were able to identify seventeen different items that were carried by the children that day, providing a list of items that could be used to identify their remains or whereabouts. However, the police's continue efforts continued to prove fruitless.

The Psychic Circus

On November 8, 1966, nearly a year after the children's initial disappearance, an internationally-renowned psychic from the Netherlands, Gerard Croiset, was flown to Australia to investigate the case. His presence caused a whirlwind of media coverage in Australia and across the world. After making a series of outlandish and ever-changing claims, Croiset claimed that the children were buried underneath a warehouse just minutes away from the children's school.

"I appreciate him (Gerard Croiset) coming out to find the children," Jim Beaumont said. "But I don't believe what he said. I don't believe the children are dead and will continue to believe until given evidence that proves otherwise."

The building, which was under construction at the time of their disappearance, was eventually razed and excavated after the owners raised $40,000 for the project as a result of public pressure. No evidence of the children or their belongings were ever found.

"The press and police followed Croiset around everywhere," Orange said. "He was an obvious con artist but they were desperate. They had nothing."

A Series of Letters

Beginning in 1968, the parents of the three children began to receive a series of letters which rekindled hope in the idea that their children may still be alive. Postmarked from Dandernong, Victoria, the series of letters claimed to be written by Jane, the eldest daughter. She claimed to be under the supervision of a man and in good health and care, saying

Dear Mum and Dad,

We had a beautiful lunch today...The man is feeding us really well. The man took us to see The Sound of Music yesterday.

Police officers believed the letters to be from Jane after comparing them to examples of her handwriting and, as far as 1981, the Sidney Morning Herald produced analysis from handwriting experts claiming that the letters were actually from the missing child.

Following receipt of the letters supposedly sent from Jane, the parents received a letter from a man claiming to be in possession of the children. He said that he was willing to hand the children over to the parents at a specific time and location. The Beaumonts arrived at the appointed time and location with an undercover police officer but no one showed. They later received a letter from the same man claiming that he saw the undercover police officer arrive with the parents and that he would now keep the children, ending any hope of a peaceful exchange.

In 1992, following another investigation and remarkable achievements in fingerprint technology, authorities identified the author of the letters as a local man who was just a teenager at the time of the hoax. He reportedly wrote and mailed the letters as "a joke."

False Closure

Then, in November 2013, South Australian police received an anonymous tip claiming that the children were buried underneath a warehouse located in North Plympton. Although radar identified "one small anomaly, which can indicate movement or objects within the soil," no evidence was ever found.

The Suspects

Bevan Spencer von Einem

Bevan Spencer von Einem has long been considered the prime suspect in the disappearance of the Beaumont children. Einem was convicted of the July 1983 murder of fifteen-year-old Richard Kelvin, son of a popular news reporter, in 1984. Police have long suspected Einem of working with a series of accomplices and of having committed other abductions and murders.

In 1983, a police informant known as "Mr. B" told police that Einem claimed to have taken three children from a beach to perform medical "experiments," claiming that he performed "brilliant surgery" on the three children before accidentally killing one of them. Following the child's accidental death, the informant stated that Einem claimed to have killed the other two children and buried them in an open field outside the city of Adelaide.

Einem did bare some resemblance to the descriptions of the tall blond man given to police following the disappearance of the Beaumont children and was known to frequent Glenely Beach to spy on people in the changing rooms. He was also noted as having an obsession with children.

Einem worked as an accountant and lived with his mother. There were rumors that he was part of a ring of Adelaide professionals who shared a "hobby" of kidnapping, drugging and raping boys.

"Einem did match the description of the police sketches," Orange said. "And he did like to frequent the same beach. He seemed more interested in young teenage males as his list of known victims would indicate. Einem was a homosexual who picked up hitchhikers with his transvestite friend where they would engage in a "rough trade" style of sex. He would take photographs of his victims as a keepsake. The three young children would seem to be outside of his modus operandi."

However, Einem was significantly younger than the suspect described by witnesses; Einem was around 20 years old at the time, while the description of the suspect placed him in his late 20s. But, in 2007 local police officers identified a young man who looked exactly like a young Einem in Channel 7 news footage of the incident taken days after the disappearance. He remains a prime suspect in the case.

"The newly found news footage does implicate Einem in a psychological way," Orange said. "Killers often like to return to the scene of the crime. He was spotted on film, days after the disappearance. What are the odds against that?"

Arthur Stanley Brown

Arthur Stanley Brown, along with Einem, is considered to be one of two prime suspects in the abduction of the Beaumont children. In 1988, Brown, then 86 years old, was charged with kidnapping, raping, and murdering Judith and Susan Mackey in Townsville, Queensland. His first trial was declared a mistrial after the jury failed to reach a verdict in the case and his second trial was blocked because he was declared unfit to stand trial; Brown was suffering from dementia and Alzheimer's disease by this time.

He is considered one of two prime suspects in the case because of his connection to the murder of other children and because of his remarkable resemblance to descriptions of the tall blond man seen with the children at the time of their disappearance. He was also a prime suspect in the Adelaide Oval case, which involved the disappearance of Joanna Ratcliffe and Kirste Gordon.

"Brown was a known pedophile by his closest family members," Orange said. "He is alleged to have molested numerous younger relatives. He could be placed in the same area and time of the Beaumont children but nothing could be proven."

Although Brown is considered to be a prime suspect in the disappearance of the Beaumont children, the suspect in the case was identified as being in his late 30s; Brown was in his 50s at the time. Brown died in 2002 without ever admitting to the crime.

"Brown would move into a nursing home at the end of his life," Orange said. "He would die an innocent man with the courts never able to officially charge him because of his Alzheimer's."

James Ryan O'Neill

James Ryan O'Neill, convicted of murdering nine-year-old Ricky John Smith in the Australian state of Tasmania in 1975 and currently serving a life sentence for the crime, was considered as a suspect in the Beaumont children disappearance for some time. He is reported as having told several friends in the early 1970s that he was responsible for the disappearance of the Beaumont children in 1966. However, he was publicly eliminated as a suspect by the South Australian police. He remains in prison in Tasmania to this day.

"O'Neill was the subject of a documentary called 'The Fishermen,'" Orange said. "In the documentary, he is evasive about being the man behind the disappearance of the children. He is, however, at the forefront of most pundits who have studied the story. While Brown and Einem did not have charming personas, O'Neill did. He was handsome and smiley with the ability to manipulate everyone around him. He could fabricate lies at the drop of a hat so it is easy to believe that he would be able to charm the children into his acquaintance. People who knew him all described him as 'the most likable man you'll ever meet.' No one could believe that he would be capable of such an act."

Derek Ernest Percy

In 2007, the Victorian newspaper The Age published a report stating that Derek Ernest Percy, at the time the longest-serving prisoner in the southeastern Australian state, was responsible for the disappearance of the Beaumont children in 1966. Initially jailed in

1970 for the 1969 murder of 12-year-old Yvonne Tuohy, Percy was found not guilty of the crime by reason of insanity, but was nonetheless jailed "indefinitely."

He is widely considered to be Australia's worst child serial killer and is suspected of the killings of the Beaumont children, as well as the abduction, attempted rape, and stabbing of Marianne Schmidt and Christine Sharrock on January 11, 1965. In October 2014, Percy was also ruled to have abducted and killed seven-year-old Linda Stilwell in 1968. However, Percy passed away from cancer in 2013, having never admitted to any of his crimes. He remains a possible suspect in the case.

"Percy is unique in that he may have had his mother not aiding him but covering up for him," Orange said. "He is certainly one of the most sadistic pedophiles on record, his doings are unmentionable out of respect for his victims. He was in the city at the time of the Beaumont children disappearance and is probably the top suspect along with O'Neill. His mother, however, has thrown out a lot of what could have been evidence in the case."

Related Cases

Two similar cases to the disappearance of the Beaumont children attracted widespread attention in the South Australian media, and the primary suspect in the Beaumont children's kidnapping case was convicted in one case and suspected in the other.

The Adelaide Oval Case

On August 25, 1972, two young girls, Joanne Ratcliffe (aged 11) and Kirste Gordon (aged 4) went missing while attending an Australian football game. They are presumed dead. This case also received widespread attention in the South Australian media and Bevan Spencer von Einem was considered the primary suspect in their disappearance.

Einem matched the descriptions of the tall blond man provided by witnesses in the Beaumont children's case and closely resembles the police sketch released to the public. A private police report in leaked in 1989 identified Einem as the primary suspect in the case.

The Family Murders

From 1973 to 1983, a group of men is believed to have been involved in the abduction, rape, and murder of a series of young men and male teenagers in the Adelaide area. Five teens were killed during this time period, including Alan Barnes (aged 16), Neil Muir (aged 25), Peter Stogneff (aged 14), Mark Langley (aged 18), and Richard Kelvin (aged 15). All victims were abducted and subjected to extended bouts of torture and physical assault, including sexual assault and medical experimentation.

Bevan Spencer von Einem was convicted of the abduction and murder of Richard Kelvin 1984 and is currently serving life in prison in Port Augusta prison. In 1990, he was also charged with the murder of Alan Barnes and Mark Langley, but key evidence from the Richard Kelvin murder was ruled inadmissible in the trial. Following the ruling against this key evidence, the prosecution dropped these charges against Einem on December 21, 1990.

Although Einem was the only member of this group to be convicted, and four out of five of The Family Murders remain unsolved, law enforcement officials believe that Einem was part of a white-collar group that preyed on young children. He remains the prime, and only living, suspect in the disappearance of the Beaumont children.

Impact on the Parents

Jim and Nancy Beaumont continued to hold out hope of finding their children for several decades after their disappearance. In fact, the couple continued to live at the Somerton Park home, at 109 Harding Street, that they shared with their children for nearly two decades, hoping that the children would return home someday. Nancy Beaumont was reported as saying that it would be "dreadful" if the children returned to the home only to find that their parents had moved.

"The Beaumonts left the rooms of the children untouched," Orange said. "Every toy, every book even the bed was left exactly as the children had left them."

The couple were never considered as suspects in the case and cooperated with the police at every turn in the investigation, including working with the police and searching in vain every time a new lead developed in the case over the next several decades.

According to The Age, the parents "have since separated, but still live in Adelaide." The stress and sorrow that resulted from their children's abduction, combined with the constant new leads and media attention is said to have contributed to the failure of their marriage.

Jim, in particular, is said to still be suffering from intense and inconsolable grief every time a new development is reported. Nancy was also reported to have suffered extreme grief and horror when, in 1990, several Australian newspapers released computer-generated images of what her children would look like after aging several decades. She reportedly refused to look at the pictures.

"Jim was a little bit stronger than Nancy," Orange said. "He would address the media more than she did. But they both suffered terribly for the rest of their lives into their eighties. They would spend over fifty years wishing for their children's return, getting false hope after false hope, one false lead after another which would all ultimately turn up nothing. It was a horrific cruelty."

Lastly, Jim and Nancy have largely been seen as sympathetic and pitiable figures in the Australian media and in society at large. Although their actions may seem reckless or irresponsible by today's standards, Australian society was viewed as extremely safe in the 1960s and their policy of allowing a child to supervise their younger siblings both in the home and in public was practiced by a large portion of Australian parents.

Impact on Australian Society

The disappearance of the Beaumont children became an overnight sensation in Australia, led to one of the largest police searches in the country's history, and remains the most famous missing persons case in the country. Prior to this incident, Australia was largely viewed as one of the safest societies on the planet and children were allowed to roam freely, doors remained unlocked at all times, and there was little fear of strangers. All of that changed overnight.

"Australia lost its innocence with the disappearance of the Beaumont Children," Orange said. "For three young children to disappear was unheard of. The city where they grew up was a dignified place, a safe place. But it was all an illusion that went away the day the children went missing."

During the initial search for the children, Jim Beaumont went on national television to appeal for their safe return. His heartfelt address to the nation had a lasting impact on the parents and children who watched his plea. Hundreds of viewers called into the station to offer tips and Australian police report that hundreds of tips continue to come in every year to this day. His image on national television continues to serve as a warning for those who believe in the incorruptibility of their fellow citizens and in the safety of their country.

"A lot of people today will blame the parents for letting them go on the bus alone," Adelaide resident Rachel Harding said. "But times were different back then. Back then kids would walk to school by themselves. Kids were told not to talk to strangers. The Beaumonts did tell their children to not talk to children. But child molesters are cunning monsters. My guess is that he may have stolen the eldest child's purse then conned them into seeing him as their benefactor. They would not have had money to get home then along comes this "blonde man" who offers them money. Buys them food and promises to take them home."

Children who came of age in Australia during the 1960s have remarked that there was a definite culture shift following the Beaumont children's disappearance, often describing a "before" and "after." While children were once allowed to roam freely and interact with strangers, Australian parents have since altered their style of parenting and curtailed the amount of freedom offered to young children.

"It was the type of case where we believe there was a lone offender," Australian police detective Des Bray said. "It isn't the type of crime where one would go around bragging about. But we do hope that he told someone and that somebody knows something."

If the Beaumont children are alive today, they would all be in their 50s and would have lived through years of hearing their names and story broadcast on national television and reported on breathlessly in national newspapers. Despite the vast amount of information we have on the case, their fates may never be known with any certainty.

Both Jim and Nancy Beaumont are still alive, and as of this writing they are ninety and eighty-years old respectively. The anonymous tips and false hopes continue to come in today as they did over fifty years ago.

THE MISSING BEAUTY QUEEN : THE DISAPPEARANCE OF TARA GRINSTEAD

AMANDA DARLING

"I'm an 11th-grade history teacher at Irwin County High school. I also have a cheerleading squad of Junior Varsity cheerleaders. I just completed my first year of teaching, and I love every bit of it." - Tara Grinstead in a 1999 interview.

Tara Grinstead was a beauty pageant winner and high school teacher who strangely disappeared on October 22nd, 2005.

The mystery of her disappearance is as baffling now as it was over ten years ago. Tara was a beautiful woman in a small town and drew the attention of many men. But as investigators peeled back the onion on her life, they discovered that she had a complex personal life, one with many lovers and layers of relationship any one of whom may have sought to do her harm out of jealousy.

Investigators have pieced together the timeline of her activities prior to her disappearance. But the missing piece lies sometime during the night of October 22nd, 2005, when someone abducted Tara Grinstead and she would never be seen again.

What happened to Tara Grinstead?

EARLY LIFE

Tara was born on November 14th, 1974 to Faye and Billy Grinstead. She grew up in Hawkinsville, Georgia and was a popular cheerleader in high school as well as a diligent student. Her parents would divorce and her father would remarry a woman named Connie to whom Tara grew close to as well.

Tara loved animals, singing and going to church as a kid.

One cannot look upon pictures and video of Tara and not remark that she had a striking beauty. Graced with a voluptuous figure and long black hair, she had the ability to light up any room she walked into. She would eventually compete in beauty pageants, falling in love with the preparation, competition, and glamor of the activity.

"She had been into so many (pageants) that I had lost count," Connie Grinstead said.

Tara meticulously prepared for the pageants, remaining physically fit, taking speech lessons and learning how to sing. She would also graduate from Middle Georgia College and become a teacher at Irwin County High School in Ocilla. She would teach history to 11th graders but not give up on her pageant hopes.

In 1999, she would achieve the first step in her dream to enter the Miss USA contest, when she would win the local title of Miss Tifton.

This victory would allow her to compete in the Miss Georgia pageant. She would also receive scholarship winnings that she would use to help pay for her continuing college education.

"It was, for her, more than a dream come true," Tara's best friend Maria Hulett said. "It was the chance for her to be really proud of herself."

Footage of Tara during the Georgia pageant showed her to be an exuberant woman with a zest for life. She loved to exercise, drink Diet Coke with grenadine, collect Barbies and listening to 80s music like Bon Jovi. She had an infectious smile and played to the camera as she showed off her yellow business suit that she would wear for the pageant interview.

"Why did you pick yellow?" the reporter asked.

"Because it shows that I'm a happy person," Tara said.

With her pageant days behind her, Tara would earn a master's degree in education from Valdosta State University.

"She wanted to be a principal," her friend Oshja Anderson said. "She was well on her way."

Always seeking to improve herself, Tara would teach classes during the day and go to graduate school at night. She also held down a part-time job selling cosmetics at the local department store. By 2005, she had applied for a doctoral program in history and would occasionally fill in as the assistant principal.

"On the surface," forensic psychiatrist Orange said. "Tara's life looked to be a stellar one. She had a bright future in academia and during her pageant days, she learned to put forward the best appearance. But what lurked underneath in her personal life is the mystery."

MARCUS HARPER

At the heart of Tara's disappearance is figuring out the type of relationships she had with the numerous men in her life. She worked as a teacher, went to night school and worked the cosmetics counter at a department store. Outgoing and bubbly, she didn't have the personality type to reject anyone out of hand. She attracted men and had many suitors.

She did have a longtime boyfriend in Marcus Harper.

Harper was an Ocilla police officer who would later become an Army Ranger. Both of Tara's parents liked him as they both expressed the fact that he always remained respectful of them. They have consistently maintained that they never witnessed Harper treating Tara with disrespect.

Tara, however, had expressed to her sister that she was afraid of Marcus.

"She said she was afraid of him," Tara's sister Anita said. "What he had gone through with the Ranger training. He was capable of anything."

"Marcus was a strong Alpha-male type," Orange said. "A cop and an Army Ranger. Tara was rumored to have dated another cop as well but she didn't appear to have a type. From what we can gather, she dated a slew of men from older to younger, and from different walks of life."

About a year prior to her disappearance, Tara had broken up with Marcus. She had given him an ultimatum and wanted to be married. He did not want marriage but wanted to remain committed. The relationship would turn sour at that point.

Tara would begin to date other people. She was in a car with a romantic suitor named Rhett Roberts who was the son of her landlord.

Marcus spotted the couple and would go ballistic, shouting obscenities at Tara.

Despite this angry confrontation, Tara would maintain ties with Marcus. In late July or early August of 2005 they would go to St. Augustine on a beach trip. After their date, Tara would confide to a friend that she was concerned about Marcus's temper.

Marcus would then be deployed back to Iraq a few weeks later. Tara would write the Army Ranger a letter in which she effectively ended their relationship.

According to Marcus, however, their relationship didn't come to a close until October of 2005. He had returned from the Middle East and called Tara to tell her that their relationship was over. Tara was at work and became so distraught that had to pull over to the side of the road. She called a friend who came and took her home. The next day, Tara would call off sick from her teaching job in order to "take a mental health day."

There was a rumor that a cop from a neighboring town, Heath Dykes, came to visit Tara at her school shortly afterward.

"These behaviors certainly show some mental fragilities on the parts of both Tara and Marcus," Orange said. "From what we can gather, it looked like an off-and-on style relationship with a few other romantic partners thrown in for good measure. It is unclear as to who was chasing who at various points of their relationship. If we are to believe Marcus, then she was chasing him. If we are to believe Tara's sister, then she was afraid of him. Why would you chase a man that you were afraid of? Something is not right here."

A few days later, Tara and Marcus would have another "heated argument" which she would tell one of her friends at her night class as well as another friend the next day while she had lunch.

According to Marcus, the argument centered around him breaking up with her. But Tara's sister Anita Gattis had a different story.

"They had a very bad argument," Anita said. "Several days before she went missing, concerning an 18-year-old that he was dating. My sister did not think that (the 18-year-old's) parents would approve of a 30-year-old dating an-18-year-old. I'm told that she threatened to tell the parents and they had a very heated argument over this."

Marcus said the argument was about something else entirely. He stated that she begged him not to end their relationship.

"She wanted me back and all," Marcus said. "And I said, 'I've started shopping outside of Ocilla, I think you need to do the same. Everybody in this town is connected to us one way or another."

"She approached me crying," Harper said as he repeated the same story on Greta Van Susteren's TV show. "She was very irrational, and she told me that if she found out I was dating someone, she would commit suicide."

But Tara's friend Osjha disputes the fact that Tara would do or say something like that.

"She's never said anything remotely similar to me ever any time."

Law enforcement authorities don't believe Tara committed suicide as she would have to go to extreme lengths to hide her own body and would have no motive to do so.

"There are a couple of contradictory things at play here," Orange said. "Tara was rumored to have dated some of her students so it would be hypocritical of her to criticize Marcus for dating someone in their teens. And it also doesn't make sense for her to come to Marcus' home begging to get back together. She had her share of suitors, some coming from out of town. She was a beautiful woman and she had options."

To her family's dismay, both the authorities and press would place Tara's life under a microscope. They had discovered that she had "several romantic relationships that occurred in relative proximity to one another."

"There was more rumors and innuendo," Orange said. "There were rumors that she was dating Rhett Roberts, her landlord's son. Rumors that she was dating one of her teenage students. Rumors that she was dating Heath Dyke, a police officer from another county. Even her own brother-in-law, Larry Gattis, was rumored to have an affair with Tara."

Both Larry and Tara's sisters are physicians. Larry specializes in geriatric medicine with only 3.3 out of 5-star reviews on Healthgrades. He was interrogated by investigators and expressed his outrage at the questions they were asking. One question was that if he had an affair with Tara and his response was judged by the polygraph as "deceptive."

ALL THAT AND A STALKER TOO...

Tara would have a stalker in a former student named Anthony Vickers. Friends recalled that Tara had taken special care to tutor Vickers but she later realized that the young man was "unstable."

"He was just kind of a troubled kid and that would be her nature," Osjha said.

Vickers was obsessed with his beauty queen teacher and claimed to have had a romantic relationship with her.

"She talked about the fact that he would call and he would rely on her and she knew it was getting too much for her," a friend named Maria said. "I just kept telling her, 'You know Tara, something's wrong."

Vickers was two years out of high school when he came to Tara's house and demanded to be let in. He pounded on the door until she called the police. Vickers resisted arrest but charges were later dropped and no restraining orders were ever filed.

The Vickers incident wasn't the only occasion that the former beauty pageant winner was being stalked. There was an incident where someone would call her home and make threats. The call was traced and it was determined to be a student in her homeroom who was promptly removed from the class.

THE NIGHT OF...

Before the night of her disappearance, Tara had enjoyed the company of her friend Dana and some teenage girls as they readied for the "Miss Georgia Sweet Potato" pageant. Her friend remembered

Tara as being in a great mood, helping out the girls with their hair and makeup. She would attend the pageant where she served as a backstage coach. Later that evening, she went to the house of a neighbor before going to a barbecue a few blocks from her home. Police believe that she had remained at the barbecue until 11 pm when she left to go home. They would find the clothes she wore at the cookout on her bedroom floor which indicated to police that she had, in fact, returned home.

From that point on, police "have no idea" what happened to Tara.

On October 24th, 2005, Tara did not show up to teach her class. Her colleagues called the police who showed up at her residence to do a welfare check. They would find her white Mitsubishi parked in the garage, unlocked. Upon entering her home, police found a business card lodged in her door.

There appeared to be no sign of forced entry. Searching through the house, police found her cell phone plugged into her charger. Her purse and keys could not be found.

Strangely, the clothes she wore the night before were piled on the bedroom floor.

Investigators found it odd that the car door was unlocked and that the car seat was pushed back. Tara was petite at only five-foot-three and would have kept the seat much closer to the steering wheel. They found an envelope of cash (one hundred dollars) on her dashboard while both her dog and cat were inside. Tara's sister said that she was an animal lover who would never just abandon her pets.

Something was wrong...

The police immediately called the Georgia Bureau of Investigation as the lacked the resources to pursue this kind of crime.

Taking over the case, the GBI believed that Tara may have left with someone that she knew, given the lack of a forced entry and the fact that only her purse and keys were missing. Neighbors did not report hearing any screaming at night.

Her disappearance shocked the small and close-knit community. To a person, Tara was described as someone who had a great personality, loved by faculty and students alike. Nothing in her professional life would suggest that she had any enemies.

Volunteers from the community immediately went to work. Irwin County students, teachers, and other townsfolk searched the area and put out flyers.

"Missing. Tara Grinstead. $20,000 Reward."

ROUNDING UP THE SUSPECTS

Longtime boyfriend Marcus Harper was one of the first to be questioned. He came with a ready-made alibi for the night of Tara's disappearance.

Marcus was seen at a bar with friends then went on a 'ride-along' with a former partner on the local police force. His whereabouts was "essentially substantiated" according to authorities.

Former student/stalker Anthony Vickers was questioned but later ruled out as a suspect. Like the others, however, he could not account for the entire thirty-four hour period when Tara was last seen and reported missing.

"Vickers is probably the only one I would rule out," Orange said. "This disappearance was too clean. Vickers was a disturbed twenty-year-old man with a crush. He would not have the emotional wherewithal or the knowledge to pull off a crime with no clues. But someone with law enforcement or medical training could."

But who left the business card behind at her door?

The card was left by Heath Dykes, a married Perry police officer with two children. He was from the next town over and had known Tara since high school.

Neighbors would tell investigators that he visited Tara's house often. It is unclear what their relationship was (outside of the obvious innuendo and rumors).

Still, he had left close to two dozen messages on Tara's answering message on the weekend she went missing.

There is small-town gossip that the two were having an affair. Local witnesses have confirmed that they saw his wife throw his clothes out on the front lawn. The content of the messages he left have not been made public but the rumors were that he was telling her "he was sorry" and that he "loved her."

What is clear is that he did call Tara's mother from the front yard and ask if she knew where Tara was and if she was alright.

Heath Dykes was the last known person at Tara's home that night as he arrived a little after midnight.

"There are simply too many secrets here," Orange said. "Something was clearly going on in Heath's mind in order for him to call Tara that many times over the course of one evening. One rumor is that they were having an affair and that she was going to tell his wife. So he was calling her in a desperate attempt to stop her from doing that. Another possibility was that she was calling him for help and he was returning her calls. His involvement led to a lot of outlandish speculation, one of which was that Heath knew that a hit man was coming for Tara and that he was calling to make sure that she was okay."

"I think the fact that she was beautiful and other people paid attention to her would obviously make some people jealous," Tara's friend Maria said. "I think she was afraid of the possibility of someone hurting her from being angry at her, having reactions to her dating people."

Numerous men were rounded up and questioned, there was Jim Perry who dated Tara years earlier, Rhett Roberts, Marcus Harper, Anthony Vickers, and Eric Cook among others.

Another unsubstantiated rumor that Tara was involved with another student named Eric Cook. A friend of his had made mention of their affair in an Internet forum post where he stated that everyone knew that they were "messing around." He also said that the police didn't make the information public out of respect for Tara's family as she dated around quite a bit. An alleged friend of Cook disputed the rumor on the forum, however. Cook would later die in a car accident.

A neighbor, Joe Poirier lived with his wife and was rumored to have been "obsessed" with Tara. The older couple admitted to "looking out for Tara" and they were fond of her. He was seen pouring concrete near his home the day after she disappeared.

Another person of interest was Larry Gattis, the brother-in-law of Tara. He was brought in for questioning after the disappearance. It would later be revealed that he had been asked if he had an affair with Tara.

Larry answered 'no'.

The polygraph machine marked it as a 'deceptive answer.'

48 HOURS

In 2008, Tara's case would be featured on the CBS News show "48 Hours Mystery." The show would illustrate the parallels between Tara's case and the disappearance of Jennifer Kesse who would go missing in Orlando, Florida three months later. The GBI would also reveal during the broadcast that they had found a latex glove in Tara's yard just a few feet away from her front porch.

The GBI forensic team would analyze the DNA left in the glove and determine that it was a man's DNA, they just do not know who it belongs to. They would compare the DNA samples of the numerous men who were associated with or knew Tara but none of them have matched.

The DNA has also been entered into the Georgia and national databases but no match has been made to date.

"The glove may be a red herring," Orange said. "Whoever entered the home left nothing behind, no prints, DNA, nothing. So it was obviously someone who knew exactly what they were doing. They wanted to harm Tara."

A HOAX AND FALSE TIPS

In February of 2009, a man calling himself the "Catch Me Killer" began posting videos boasting that he had murdered sixteen women. One of the women he described had a close resemblance to Tara Grinstead. The man producing the video digitally obscured his face and voice but police eventually identified the culprit as twenty-seven-year-old Andrew Haley.

Haley performed the videos as part of a bizarre hoax and was eliminated as a possible suspect.

Investigator Gary Rothwell has expressed his lament at how the rumors and speculation have caused unfair stress to many who have been already tried in the public eye. "Irresponsible public accusations have been made about them, and they have no way to respond or defend themselves. And it's frustrating that we don't have evidence to rule anyone in or out."

Rothwell admits, however, that he has information that has not been released.

In February of 2015, authorities acted on a tip which led them to drain a pond in Fitzgerald, Georgia.

They didn't go into details as to what the specifics of the tip were. The pond would be drained and nothing would be found.

ALIBIS

Police have alibis from all the men who knew Tara Grinstead but no one has been ruled out because no one can account for the full thirty-four hour period.

Rhett Reynolds stated he went to sleep after the cookout. Joe Poirier was with his wife next door.

The most elaborate alibi, however, came from Marcus Harper.

Again, Marcus was in a local bar and a friend of Tara's had spotted him there. She would call Tara at around 10:15 and 10:30 to tell Tara that Marcus was there.

After 1 am, Marcus left the bar and went to look for his police officer friend, Sgt. Sean Fletcher. Fletcher was on duty that night.

Fletcher knew Tara as well. Ironically, he was one of the officers who arrived at Tara's house when Anthony Vickers, Tara's former student, was banging on her door.

There were rumors that Tara didn't like Fletcher because he had told Harper that Tara was entertaining Heath Dykes at her home.

Fletcher would deny that speculation.

"What we can extrapolate from this scenario was that Vickers was angry that his crush, Tara, was with another man," Orange said. "So he goes to her home and demands that she talk to him. He's young, twenty-years-old, and doesn't understand why she would do this to him. He is then arrested by Fletcher who relays what Tara is doing to Marcus, a man that Tara is wary about because of his temper. So now we have more than just a love triangle, it is a love octagon, with numerous men vying for and getting jealous over the attention of Tara."

At around 1:49 am, Fletcher received a call from dispatch informing him that Marcus Harper was looking for him. The two met up and walked Fletcher's beat, checking doors in downtown Ocilla.

Around 2:45, Fletcher was dispatch to a home where a mentally unbalanced man, Bennie Merritt, had stumbled into a home and refused to leave. Marcus would join Fletcher on the call as did two other officers. Merritt, however, was gone from the premises.

Minutes later, they began to search for Merritt who was also a neighbor of Tara's. The drunken Merritt would accost the cashier at the local gas station then be apprehended. Both Fletcher and Harper had responded to the call at the gas station and by the time they were done it was 4:28 am.

Marcus then headed home.

Investigators would later be able to corroborate these details with multiple witnesses, including Merritt, who was scrutinized as a possible suspect in the kidnapping as well.

Marcus Harper, however, has not been ruled out as a potential person of interest in the case.

"Marcus's alibi is too perfect," GBI investigator Maurice Godwin said.

Both Larry and Anita Gattis believe that Marcus is the top suspect.

"He had the motive," Tara's sister said. "And the training."

The insinuation would draw the ire of Marcus who became upset that Anita consistently brought up his military and police training. He continues to deny any involvement in Tara's disappearance.

"I don't wanna hurt any innocent civilian much less someone I spent five and a half years of my life with."

"What is clear is that there isn't a whole lot forthcoming about Tara's personal life to draw the conclusions we need to about who is the most probable suspect," Orange said. "Like in the Natalee Holloway case, the sexual activity of the woman in question is kept hidden. If her background reveals that she was a promiscuous woman, there will e less sympathy and urgency to solve the crime. That is one of the more striking aspects of the case, aside from Tara's vanishing, is the cover-up of Tara's personal life in order to protect her reputation."

UNSOLVABLE CASE?

Tara Grinstead's case is still being investigated. The GBI reports that they receive numerous leads per day, most of which are false.

Her body has never been found but her impact on the lives of those around her and her students will never be forgotten.

"I'm so sorry to hear about what happened to Miss Grinstead," said Christine Kang, a South Korean exchange student from Grinstead's class. "She is so caring and giving to her students. I am sure she will come home soon safely. I will pray for her every night."

THE MURDER OF BROOKE WILBERGER

58

OLIVIA WATSON

Chapter 1

May 24, 2004 is a day many people in Corvallis, Oregon will never forget. It was the day a drunk man who was also high on crack set forth to destroy a life. Joel Courtney set out that morning in his 1997 green Dodge Caravan in search of a young, pretty co-ed to fulfill his dark fantasies. He cruised through the Oregon State University campus, searching, failing. But Courtney was persistent, and his wishes were soon fulfilled after he came across the Oak Park apartment complex a block down the road.

On the same morning, Brooke Wilberger woke up without any inclination that this might be her final day on Earth. She was newly home after finishing her first year of University, and was enjoying how sunny the spring had turned out to be. She headed over to the Oak Park apartment complex, which her sister managed, to help do some cleaning and basic repairs. Her sister needed help washing the lightposts out in the parking lot, so Wilberger grabbed some rags and a bucket of soapy water and got to work.

A few minutes into her work, Wilberger noticed a green van pull up. Inside, a man was waving an envelope at her, trying to get her attention. He looked like he needed help, so Wilberger approached. When the van pulled away seconds later, all that was left of Brooke was the soapy water and her now-broken flip flops.

It would be more than five years before Brooke Wilberger came home, but she would never come home alive. The story of her disappearance was a twisted tale full of hope, but it would only ever have a bittersweet ending.

Chapter 2

Brooke Wilberger was born in Fresno, California on February 20, 1985. She was the youngest of six. With three older sisters and two older brothers, she lived in a busy household, but it was a pleasant place to live. Her parents, Greg and Cammy Wilberger, were devout Mormons, and raised their children to be the same. The family was incredibly close-knit.

Brooke Wilberger grew to be quite a beautiful, accomplished young woman. Besides boasting a strong set of mormon morals, she also excelled in school and had a lot of friends. The tall, thin blonde also received a lot of attention from the guys in her school, but she seldom dated.

The summer before Brooke began high school, the Wilberger family left California behind and moved North to Eugene, Oregon. Here, Brooke attended Elmira High School, and met her first serious boyfriend, Justin Blake. Blake also came from a mormon family, and was devoted to his religion, so the couple got along famously. They respected each other's minds, bodies, and faith.

The young couple graduated together in 2003, and while they were both dedicated to each other, they were on different paths towards the future. Wilberger wanted to go right to college so she could better equip herself with the knowledge she would need to turn around and better those in need around her. Blake was ready to jump into missionary work.

Wilberger was accepted into the Brigham Young University in Provo, Utah, and when she set off for her freshman year there, Blake set off for Venezuela to participate in a Mormon missionary campaign.

Although she was separated from her first love, Wilberger could not deny how happy she was at Brigham Young. The University was owned and operated by the Church of Jesus Christ of Latter Day Saints, and was the largest religious university in the country. She was immersed in her faith in new experiences and knowledge. She was actively participating in something much larger than herself, and she loved it.

Wilberger kept in constant contact with her family while away at University. She would often call and tell them about what she was learning, who she was meeting, and what she was doing. Her favorite topic of conversation, though, was always the inspiration her surroundings gave her to do better for the world. Although she was excited to see her family after the end of the year, she was in no rush to leave the busy, bustling campus for small-town Oregon.

After finishing her classes for the year, Brooke returned home to her family in late April of 2004. Her parents still lived in Eugene, but she wanted to maintain some of her freedom, so Brooke often stayed with her sister, Stephanie, who lived an hour outside of Eugene in an apartment complex she managed in Corvallis.

Her family were ecstatic to have her back home, close by, where they believed she would be safe.

Chapter 3

On May 24, 2004, Brooke had been home for about a month. She was staying with her sister in the Oak Park apartments, which were just down the road from Oregon State University, where summer classes were already in full swing.

That morning, a female student of Oregon State named Randy was walking through the Reser Stadium parking lot when she noticed a green van driving around her. When it pulled up next to her, the driver of the van got out and asked Randy for directions. The student had a bad feeling about the man, and when she looked in the back seat of the van she noticed a bunch of empty boxes and blankets. Before the man could get too close, Randy excused herself and hurried off to class.

Several minutes later, another student, Crystal, was approached by the same van in the same parking lot. Crystal did speak to the man, who again asked for directions, but the conversation was interrupted by an athletic's coach, who Randy had reported the earlier incident to. When confronted by the coach, the van's driver quickly jumped back into his vehicle and sped off of the campus.

While this was all happening, Brooke Wilberger was a block down the road from Reser Stadium at the Oak Park apartment complex. That morning she was planning on helping her sister Stephanie do some routine maintenance work on the complex. She decided to start with washing the lamp posts in the parking lot, so she grabbed a bucket, filled it with soapy water, and headed outside. Stephanie saw Brooke hard at work scrubbing the lamp posts at 10:00 a.m. It was the last time she ever saw her sister alive.

Shortly after 10:00 a.m., the same green van that had been causing havoc on the Oregon State campus pulled into the Oak Park apartment complex. The van pulled up to Brooke, blocking her view of the apartments. He began asking for directions, but when Brooke drew near, he pulled out a knife and forced the 19-year-old into the back seat of his van and sped away.

Five minutes down the road, the van pulled over and it's driver, Joel Courtney, got out and bound Wilberger's arms and legs with duct tape. He also covered her body with blankets he had stashed in the back seat. After this, he sped off towards a nearby area that was covered with heavy forestation.

Hours after Brooke was snatched from the apartment complex, her sister Stephanie realized that she hadn't seen or heard from her in a while. She decided to track her down to make sure she was okay, and began with the place she had last seen her—the complex's parking lot. When she got there she was surprised to see an almost empty parking lot, save for the cleaning supplies Brooke had been using and Brookes flip flop sandals, one of which was now broken.

Stephanie immediately ran inside and called police, who immediately launched a missing person's case despite their protocol stating they should wait 24-hours first. Brooke's broken flip flops at her last known location triggered enough of an alarm.

When detectives arrived at the Oak Park apartments, they quickly discovered that her truck, purse, phone, and wallet were all still at the apartments. If she had left the apartments by herself, she had done so without any identification, money, and shoes. It seemed unlikely that this would have been the case.

The search for Brooke began in the same way most crimes do—with the victim's significant other. In this case, Brooke's long-term boyfriend was quickly eliminated because he was over 4000 miles away doing missionary work in Venezuela. Brooke's family was also quickly ruled out.

During this process, the word of Brooke's disappearance quickly got out to the community, and a massive volunteer search was launched by the Wilberger's Mormon church. Within days of Brooke's disappearance, both Eugene and Corvallis were covered in missing posters detailing Brooke's physical appearance and last known location. Over 4000 acres of heavily-wooded area outside of Corvallis was searched for any signs of the missing girl over eleven days. None were found.

Police soon began to realize that the best chance they had of finding Wilberger would be to find the person who had taken her from the Oak Park apartments, so they quickly began to focus on the few early leads they had in the case.

The method in which Wilberger was abducted led police to believe that her abductor was a repeat offender. It's difficult to grab a grown woman off of the streets without anyone seeing or hearing anything. Police began looking through sex offender registries and crime logs to create a suspect pool, one that turned out to include over one thousand names, all of whom were interviewed.

One of the first people contacted by police was 45-year-old ex-con Lauren Hugo Krueger. He had been convicted in 1985 for attempted rape and had served time for the felony assault and kidnapping of a 23-year-old jogger. Krueger had also been questioned in relation to several reports of harassment and stalking. Most damningly, Krueger had also been spotted at a car dealership less than a block away from where Wilberger was abducted from. It was a promising start to the investigation.

Chapter 4

Many police officers in Corvallis believed they may have identified the man who abducted Brooke Wilberger on May 24, 2004, as being Lauren Krueger. He had committed several similar crimes in the past, making him a likely suspect. However, when he was interviewed, police discovered he had an airtight alibi for that afternoon, and he was eliminated in the case.

Shortly after Krueger was eliminated as a suspect, another man by the name of Sun Koo King was identified as a probably suspect. King was an Oregon State graduate who was unemployed and lived in the area. He had recently had a lot of trouble with the law for breaking and entering into Oregon State dorm rooms and stealing their occupants underwear.

Detectives searched King's home and found a startling collection of women's underwear, used tampons, and pubic hair. King also catalogued where he found each object of his collection, which allowed investigators to see that he had gotten most of the items from dorms at the University and from the laundry room at the Oak Park apartments, the same apartments Brooke Wilberger lived in with her sister.

Police were shocked by what they found at King's home, but what shocked them more was that there seemed to be no sign of Brooke Wilberger anywhere. Further, King passed a polygraph test and seemed to have an airtight alibi. Investigators were again forced to abandon the promising lead.

By October 2004, five months after Brooke's disappearance, police had a third strong suspect—Aeryn Evans. Evans had been arrested the month before for attacking a Oregon State student on campus. Evans' step sister called police after the incident suspecting that he may have been involved in Wilberger's disappearance too, but this was quickly discovered to be impossible by police.

Frustrated by having to eliminate three great suspects in a row, police decided they needed to take a different approach in the hunt for Wilberger's abductor. They decided to focus in on the one piece of evidence they had directly connected to the person who took Brooke—a green Dodge Caravan.

Police suspected that the green van was connected to Brooke's disappearance because of the two earlier reports from Randy and Crystal on the Oregon State campus, as well as from a tip call from a man who identified himself as Brian. Brian told police that he had seen a green van driving around the area Brooke was last seen. The driver was acting suspicious enough that the van had stood out to the man. The three incidents were too bizarre for police not to connect with Brooke's disappearance on the same day.

Both Randy and Crystal were interviewed by police, but neither were able to give a clear description of the van's driver. They had both been too spooked at the time. However, the coach that had intervened in Crystal's encounter with the van had gotten a good look at the van itself and was able to provide police with more details, including the fact that the van had had Minnesota license plates.

While police were now convinced that the van seen on the Oregon State University was the van used in Wilberger's abduction, they still had no idea where to find the van, and no idea who had been driving it. By November, 2004, six months after Brooke's abduction, investigators assigned to the case were still on square one. Little did they know though, that another crime was about to be committed in Albuquerque, New Mexico, and this crime would lead them right to Wilberger's killer.

Chapter 5

On November 29, 2004, a 22-year-old Russian exchange student, who goes by the pseudonym Natalie Kirov, left the daycare she worked at on the University of New Mexico campus for home. Minutes away from her doorstep, a car pulled up next to her and a man jumped out and told her to get into the car. Terrified, she complied.

The man held Kirov captive in his car at knifepoint as he drove off. When they got to a secluded area of a dead end road, the man pulled the car over and began to sexually assault the young woman, forcing her to remove her clothes in the process.

After sexually assaulting the Russian beauty, the man declared that he needed a drug fix, a "pick-me-up," and drove to a shady apartment complex to purchase some crack. He left Kirov in his car, bound up with her own shoelaces. While her captor was inside, Kirov managed to free her hands and unlock the car. She immediately ran into the street, despite being mostly naked, and flagged down a passing car.

Just as Kirov settles into the car she flagged down her captor emerged from the nearby apartment. After seeing how terrified Kirov became, her saviours quickly drove off in the opposite direction and brought her to the police station. She was finally safe.

Police immediately responded to Kirov's report by visiting the apartments her attacker stopped in to buy his drugs. They were able to find a lady willing to admit that a guy named Joel matching Kirov's description had stopped by earlier that night. Further, she knew where Joel lived.

Police immediately proceeded to the address given to them and immediately spotted the red car Kirov described parked in the lot outside. Police had just begun examining the vehicle when they were approached by a man who said he owned the car. Police asked him if his name was Joel, and he immediately responded yes. Police responded in turn by arresting him.

The Joel police now had in custody was Joel Courtney—a 38-year-old mechanic fisherman. Joel lived in Albuquerque with his wife and three children, but his marriage was incredibly unstable. Only a few weeks before this arrest, Courtney's wife had taken out a restraining order on him.

When police dug deeper into Courtney's past, they discovered that he had a long standing drug problem that they were able to trace back to his childhood in Beaverton, Oregon. Courtney had grown up an average, loving family, but his life began deteriorating after he started using drugs at the tender age of 11. By the age of 14, Courtney began repeatedly molesting his sister and cousins, and by the age of 19, he began experimenting with satanism, and was arrested several times for sexual assaults.

Now, many years later, he was back in custody for the sexual assault of Natalie Kirov, but it had been almost 20 years since he had been committed a crime, something Albuquerque detectives were skeptical of. They wondered if he had victimized any other women who crossed his path over the years, so they contacted authorities in Oregon, Courtney's home state, to ask if there were any unsolved crimes that matched Courtney's modis operandi. Almost immediately, Oregon police mentioned the disappearance of Brooke Wilberger six months ago, hoping to finally provide some answers to Wilberger's family and the surrounding communities.

Chapter 6

After having Joel Courtney brought to their attention, the Brooke Wilberger taskforce in Corvallis, Oregon decided to look further into Courtney's past to see if they could connect him to Wilberger's disappearance. They were quickly rewarded for this decision.

Investigators soon found out that Courtney and his wife had only recently moved to Albuquerque, New Mexico. Before that, the couple moved around Oregon frequently looking for cheap accommodations. At the time of Wilberger's disappearance, the couple were living with relatives in Portland, Oregon, an hour's drive away from Corvallis.

Further, investigators found that Courtney had been working for a janitorial company in Corvallis while he lived in Portland. He drove the company's 1997 green Dodge Caravan with Minnesota license plates to and from work each day.

Courtney's van was the exact van police had been trying to track down for the last several months. Armed with this knowledge, police managed to track down the vehicle, which was immediately brought to Portland to be searched for any forensic evidence that may have survived. Specifically, they were looking for any DNA evidence to compare to known samples of Brooke Wilberger and Joel Courtney himself.

While investigators waited for the DNA results to come back from the lab, they looked into Courtney's whereabouts the day Brooke Wilberger disappeared. They discovered that Joel Courtney had actually been expected in court to face a DUI charge that very day.

Police learned that on this day Courtney apparently made a call from Corvallis saying he would be late for his court time, but he never appeared. Police also learned that the next day, a disheveled Courtney had shown up at a family member's house 16-hours away from Corvallis. When asked why he was in such a state, Courtney came up with a story of how he ran into a gang of men in the woods who had captured a young woman and forced him to do terrible things he did not want to do. Amazingly, the family member chalked the unbelievable story to Courtney's chronic drug use, and never asked about it again.

On the one-year anniversary of Brooke Wilberger's disappearance, Corvallis investigators finally received the results of the forensic sweep of the green Dodge Caravan. It was worth the wait.

The evidence recovered from the van conclusively proved that not only had both Brooke Wilberger and Joel Courtney been in the green van, but Joel Courtney had been the person to place Wilberger there, and he likely knew where she was now. The final challenge investigators now had was getting Courtney to reveal this information so they could finally bring Brooke home.

Chapter 7

On August 2, 2005, Joel Courtney, who is preparing to go on trial for the kidnap and sexual assault of Natalie Kirov is served an arrest warrant for the kidnap and presumptive murder of Brooke Wilberger. Weeks later, the Kirov case is brought to trial, and faced with the indisputable evidence against him, Courtney pleaded guilty. He was given a sentence of 18 years in prison.

But Joel Courtney didn't have long to get settled in the New Mexico prison system. In April of 2008, he was extradited to Oregon in order to stand on trial for the charges laid against him in Brooke Wilberger's case.

When the trial began in Spring of 2009, the prosecutors in the case showed the court Joel Courtney's long standing history of sexual assaults against women, which dated back to his late teen years. They also presented a witness that had seen Courtney the night before Wilberger's abduction. This individual stated that they used to work together, and that they had spent the night of May 23, 2004, drinking and smoking crack together.

Although prosecutors had a large amount of evidence against Courtney, they were missing something very important, something desired not only by them but also by Wilberger's family and the entire community of Corvallis and Eugene—Brooke.

Up to this point, investigators had been unable to find any indication of Brooke's final resting place, and Courtney wasn't about to give this information up easily. The Wilberger family was all but begging the prosecutors and investigators working on Brooke's case to make a deal with Courtney so they could bring their daughter home and give her a peaceful burial.

The District Attorney eventually succumbed to the Wilbergers' wishes and presented a plea deal to Joel Courtney. The terms of the plea deal stated that Courtney needed to plead guilty to all charges against him and reveal the location of Brooke's remains. In exchange, Courtney would receive life in prison without parole.

Courtney rejected this initial offer, but quickly returned to the bargaining table. Courtney offered to plead guilty to the crime if he could be locked up in New Mexico near his family instead of in Oregon. He also promised to reveal the location of Brooke Wilberger's remains. Courtney's counter-offer was accepted and signed.

To uphold his side of the plea deal, Joel Courtney drew a map to Brooke's burial site for investigators and walked them through the events of May 24, 2004. He told investigators the story of how he forced the young woman into his van and took her to some nearby woods to sexually assault her. After being raped, Wilberger became enraged, and tried to fight her way to freedom. Courtney responded by punching Wilberger until she fell unconscious before beating her to her certain death with a piece of wood he found nearby.

Based on this confession, and armed with Courtney's map, investigators drove 10 miles outside of Corvallis to a heavily wooded area known as the Coast Range. Their goal: to locate Brooke's remains.

After several days of searching, investigators were finally able to locate Brooke Wilberger's remains in a shallow grave next to a clearing of trees. Her grave was hidden beneath a mound of tree branches and leaves. For the Wilbergers, the news was bittersweet. They finally knew what happened to their daughter, and they finally could bring her home, but up until this point they had always maintained hope that when she came home she would still be alive.

Joel Courtney was formally sentenced to life in prison without parole two months later, and was brought back to a New Mexico prison where he prepared to spend the rest of his days. It was the end of a violent sexual predator's freedom, but most importantly, it was the end of the mystery that had plagued Oregon police and Brooke Wilberger's friends and family for years.

Brooke was finally home and at peace, and the world was a little safer now with Joel Courtney now behind bars. This is little solace to those who continue to miss Brooke Wilberger dearly, but having some answers is inarguably better than none. Those who knew Brooke in life remember her as the sweet, caring angel she was. She had a good soul in her heart and a good head on her shoulders and would have undoubtedly achieved great things in life.

Brooke's family still keep in contact with the investigators that dedicated their time to bringing Brooke home—they attend the officers' retirement parties and exchange the occasional email—a small token of the gratitude they will always hold.

THE KIDNAPPING OF BOBBY GREENLEASE

NATHAN NIXON

The Bobby Greenlease Kidnapping

The story of Bobby Greenlease is that of a tragedy. This young boy was taken from the one place a child should always feel safe; a school. The heart of the collective world was shattered while witnessing the terrible, sickening events that were unfolding. Only monsters could do such terrible things. Who would do this? How could someone stoop to this level? Most importantly, why would someone resort to this? In 1950's rural America, crimes like this just didn't happen. The turmoil that would ensue after this horrible act is one of confusion, betrayal, and heart sinking results. An innocent boy was gone much too soon, and two senseless criminals were gone much too late.

The day was September 28, 1953. A school for small children in Kansas City, Missouri was having a normal day. Classrooms were filled with young children learning the basics for their futures. Children filed in by the dozens, eagerly greeted by the smiling, caring faces of the teachers they all had learned to trust and love. This was the essence of the French Institute of Notre Dame De Sion. This was the place of learning for six year old Bobby Greenlease.

In 1953, the level of school security was vastly lower than it is today. Teachers and administration alike were much more trusting of the adults that would interact on a daily basis with children. When a mysterious woman came through the front door of the school at 10:55 A.M. that morning, there was little more than a few questions of her intentions. This mystery woman explained that she was there to pick up Robert Cosgrove Greenlease Jr. In the routine of any school, teachers and office personnel quickly learn the family and caregivers of each of their students. Needless to say, there was some suspicion of this woman who had never before been through the doors of this school and most certainly had never had any interactions with Bobby Greenlease.

The mystery woman was very anxious. She was described later as "fidgety and nervous" by school personnel. She told them that the situation was dire. She explained that she was Bobby's aunt and that his mother had suffered a catastrophic heart attack. Bobby's mother was in the hospital and he needed to come with her at once. While the school personnel were quite suspicious, it was Bobby who quelled their worry. Bobby was pulled from class at approximately 11:05 A.M. and brought to the front of the school. The mystery woman got down on a knee in front of Bobby and quickly explained that he needed to come with her.

The innocence of Bobby Greenlease is ultimately what this woman was able to take advantage of. Bobby was a trusting little boy. He learned from his daily interactions to listen to the adults around him. His parents would later explain how he was such an easygoing little boy who never gave them problems. He was described by his teacher as happy and always striving to please. For Bobby, when an adult told him to do something, he did it. He trusted them, and he had learned at a young age that he was to do as he was told. Little Bobby Greenlease always did what he was told, and he always did it with a beautiful, contagious smile on his face.

Bobby took the hand of this mysterious woman quickly after she explained what had happened. The worries of school personnel were quelled by seeing the reaction of Bobby. Surely, they thought, he wouldn't seem so eager to go with this woman if he didn't know her. With that, Bobby Greenlease left the French Institute of Notre Dame De Sion with his "aunt." Sister Moreland later recalled that "Bobby went to her with no hesitation. As they walked out of the front door, she had one arm around his shoulder and the other one holding his hand. They entered into an awaiting taxi cab. Bobby showed no fear or withdrawal from her. Everything appeared as normal."

At around 11:30 A.M. a school official, Sister Marthanna, called the Greenlease home to learn the condition of Mrs. Greenlease. To her surprise, Mrs. Greenlease answered the phone. The conversation quickly alerted the school that the story was false. Mrs. Greenlease was terrified and immediately called her husband, Robert Cosgrove Greenlease Sr. As he rushed home from work, Mrs. Greenlease alerted the Kansas City police chief. The police chief alerted the FBI of the matter. In the span of just thirty minutes, it was clear that little Bobby Greenlease, full trusting and carrying the innocence that any six year old boy would, had been kidnapped by a mystery woman. A tragedy of epic proportions was unfolding. The events of this day would go on to grip the nation in a sickening, winding road of horror and greed. The investigation was on. The Greenlease family would not have to wait long for answers.

Being as the woman who had left with Bobby had entered a cab, the first job of investigators was to track down the cab driver. Later in the day, police tracked down Willard Pearson Creech. He was a cab driver working for the Toedman Cab Company of Kansas City, Missouri. He was fully compliant with police. He informed investigators that just before 11:00 A.M. a woman entered into his cab asking to be taken to the French Institute of Notre Dame De Sion. The description Creech gave fit that of the woman who had taken Bobby Greenlease. Before the woman exited the cab, she instructed Creech to wait for her outside the school. She had said that she also needed to be taken to the Katz Drug Store at Main and Westport in Kansas City. According to Willard, it was approximately 11 minutes later that the woman came out of the school with the young boy. The boy fit the description of Bobby Greenlease. The last time that Willard Pearson Creech saw the pair, they had stopped in the rear of an early 1950's blue Sedan with Kansas license plates.

The question that was being asked by everyone was why? Why would someone kidnap an innocent six year old boy? How could someone take a child from their school? These questions would be answered very quickly. What happens next sends a chill throughout the Greenlease household.

The first ransom letter arrives just hours after the kidnapping of Bobby. The Greenleases received a letter that was postmarked 6:00 P.M. and designated for special delivery. The letter made the intentions of the kidnappers apparent. The letter stated the demand of $600,000 to be placed in a duffle bag with no bills larger than $20. The ransom would be the largest, for that time, in the history of the United States. The kidnappers ended the letter by promising the safe return of Bobby Greenlease within just 24 hours. This was contingent upon receiving all of the demanded ransom money with no sneaky tricks attempted by investigators. This was the first of many ransom contacts by the kidnappers. Investigators say they received as many as six ransom letters and 15 phone calls. The next ransom letter, however, proved to be even more chilling than the first.

The next communication between the kidnappers and the Greenleases was a letter sent on September 29, 1953. It was postmarked 9:30 P.M. and again sent special delivery. The letter, however, accompanied the Jerusalem medal of which Bobby always wore. This terrified Bobby's parents. The letter again called for $600,000 to be given for the safe return of little Bobby. The kidnappers said that "Bobby was safe, but was becoming quite homesick and wanted to see his mommy."

Within days, the story of Bobby Greenlease had attracted national media attention. The nation collectively shared the grief of the Greenlease family and hoped wholeheartedly for the safe return of Bobby. People could not understand how someone could bring themselves to take a little boy from his school. Moreover, people could not wrap their minds around how the school could let this happen. How could a six year old boy be allowed to leave with a stranger of which the school had never seen before? Many more questions would be asked. The frightening answers would soon rise to the forefront of an investigation that had only just begun.

The final communication from the kidnappers was a phone call at 1:00 A.M. on October 5, 1953. The call came directly to the Greenlease residence. The kidnappers assured the family that Bobby was safe. They stated that they had received the ransom money and that Bobby would be released within 24 hours. This was the last time that the Greenleases would hear any correspondence from the kidnappers.

Carl Hall and Bonnie Heady never had any intentions to return Bobby Greenlease to his family. The grim details of the events that took place would soon be uncovered.

Bonnie Heady was they "mystery woman" who took Bobby Greenlease from Notre Dame De Sion. She had taken Bobby, by taxi, for a few miles where they would meet up with Carl Austin Hall. Bonnie and Bobby would get into a Plymouth station wagon with Carl where they traveled to Johnson County, Kansas. It was here where authorities say Carl Hall shot little Bobby Greenlease to death with a Smith and Wesson .38 caliber revolver.

Robert Cosgrove Greenlease Sr. paid the ransom money in full to the kidnappers. They were completely unaware that Bobby had been murdered on the day of the abduction. At the time, the $600,000 was the largest ransom ever paid in the United States. Upon receiving the ransom money, Carl Hall and Bonnie Heady drove 380 miles to St. Louis, Missouri. Hall became extremely paranoid all the while. He was certain that authorities were closing in on them. He decided to try to divert attention away from the area.

On October 5, Hall purchased a pair of metal suitcases to store the ransom money. He left the duffle bag in an ash pit near St. Louis. Hall had an apartment he had rented in St. Louis on Arsenal Street. In the late hours of October 5, Carl and Bonnie arrived at the apartment.

It is important to note that Bonnie Heady and Carl Hall were heavy drug and alcohol abusers. While not the only motive for the crime, it would explain the unthinkable acts committed by the pair of criminals. Bonnie Heady was a heavy heroin user. Carl Hall would take advantage of this for his own attempted escape.

When Hall and Heady arrived at his apartment, Bonnie was heavily intoxicated. Within minutes, she had fallen asleep in the apartment. This was exactly what Carl had wanted to happen. As soon as she was asleep, Carl took the ransom money and left. He had left his accomplice to the murder of Bobby Greenlease with just $2,000 of the ransom money. He placed the money in her purse and bolted out of the door. The pair had separated on October 5, 1953.

On October 6, Hall went to a local hardware store where he purchased two garbage cans and a shovel. Growing increasingly suspicious of authorities finding out who he was and tracking him down, he acquired a rental car that morning. He drove to the Meramec River in St. Louis County and anxiously looked for a suitable place to bury the ransom money. This proved unsuccessful. He ditched the empty garbage cans and made his way back to the Coral Courts Motel, where he had been staying. By this time the paranoia of Hall was destroying his mind. He became suspicious of other motel patrons that afternoon, and decided to leave the hotel and get a room at the Townhouse Hotel in St. Louis. This would prove costly.

On the afternoon of October 6 at approximately 3:30 P.M. St. Louis police received a call from John Oliver Hager. Hager was a driver for the Ace Cab Company in St. Louis. His information led to the arrest of Carl Hall on the evening of October 6, 1953 at the Townhouse Hotel where he had checked in earlier in the day. Had Hall stayed put at the Coral Courts Motel, he may have never been discovered by Hager. When police arrested Hall, he told them that his name was John James Byrne. This was obviously fictional, but perhaps was a last gasp for freedom. Later on that evening, Hall led police to Arsenal Street to his apartment where Bonnie Heady was staying. Police entered the residence in the late hours of October 6 and arrested Heady. The pair of kidnappers were in police custody.

This began a process of interrogations by the FBI. Hall was interrogated numerous times and put together an illustration of his involvement in the crime. He insisted that all of the $600,000 ransom money was in his possession. Carl Hall admitted to several allegations against him. He admitted to his part in the kidnapping of Bobby.

He admitted to actually planning and executing the kidnapping. He also admitted to burying the body of Bobby Greenlease on Heady's property. He even admitted to picking up the ransom money that was set in the requested duffle bag. He did not, however, admit to the actual killing of Bobby Greenlease. This, as he claimed, was carried out by one Tom Marsh.

Carl Hall described a grand scheme that he agreed to with a man named Tom Marsh. He described that, once he and Heady kidnapped Bobby Greenlease, they had given the boy over to Tom Marsh. The couple was to act as the "middle men" in a scheme to extort money from Robert Cosgrove Greenlease Sr. Carl Hall argued that Tom Marsh had killed Bobby, and it was only then that he agreed to bury the body in the shallow grave by the porch of Bonnie Heady's house. The investigators didn't buy it. After more interrogation, Carl reluctantly admitted that he and Bonnie Heady were the only involved parties in the kidnapping and subsequent murder of Bobby Greenlease.

The body of Bobby Greenlease was discovered by police the next day, October 7th, 1953 at 1201 South 38th Street in St. Joseph, Missouri. At approximately 8:40 A.M. police quickly came across the shallow grave while investigating the residence of Bonnie Heady. The body was discovered buried near the front corner of the porch. The little boy's body was wrapped in plastic bags and covered in lime. The Greenlease requested their dentist to positively identify the body. At 1:05 P.M. on October 7, it was officially determined by DNA and dental records to be the body of Robert Cosgrove Greenlease Jr. Bobby's body had been found.

Upon full examination of the house, investigators found heavy blood stains on the basement floor as well as the steps entering the Heady house. Blood stains were also found on two separate fiber rugs as well as a nylon blouse. This gave the indication to police that the body had been moved several times. In addition to the blood stains, several .38 caliber shell casings were found in the house. The FBI criminal investigation lab, after much testing, determined the casings had been fired from a .38 caliber snub nose Smith and Wesson revolver. This same revolver had been found in Carl Hall's possession at the time of his arrest. FBI investigators also determined that a lead bullet found in the floor board of a Plymouth station wagon owned by Bonnie Heady was also fired from the same revolver. They now had hard evidence, along with a near full confession, to indict Carl Hall and Bonnie Heady for the murder of Bobby Greenlease.

It was not until October 11, 1953 that the full story would come out. Carl Hall told investigators the events of Bobby Greenleases murder in full, gruesome detail. He explained that he and Bonnie Heady had taken the victim from Kansas City, Missouri to Overland Park, Kansas. This, he said, was the same day that they had kidnapped Bobby from school. It was a town just outside Kansas City. This is the location where Carl Hall murdered six year old Bobby Greenlease by firing multiple rounds from his .38 caliber Smith and Wesson revolver into the child. Carl Hall then explained that they then transported the body of Bobby 45 minutes away to St. Joseph, Missouri. He then buried the body near the porch in a shallow grave and proceeded to plant flowers on it.

Bonnie Heady subsequently admitted to assisting Carl Hall with the ransom letters. She admitted to providing the instructions of the ransom money drop off to the Greenlease family. She also admitted to being the "mystery woman" who picked up Bobby Greenlease from school on the morning of September 28, 1953. She told investigators of the ruse that she had planned to use to convince school officials into letting her have Bobby.

Carl Hall and Bonnie Heady were tried on October 30, 1953. This was just over a month after their kidnapping and murder of Bobby Greenlease. Judge Albert L. Reeves presided over the case in federal court in St. Louis, Missouri. Both Hall and Heady entered guilty pleas. Shortly after, on November 19, 1953, the jury deliberated for just one hour and eight minutes. They had heard all of the gruesome details of the case. By this time, the nation was gripped on the case. Each day, updates would be put in each city newspaper. Everyone was engulfed in the proceedings. When testimony came out that the couple had planned this disgusting act well in advance, the nation's collective voice screamed for the death penalty. On November 19, 1953, both Carl Hall and Bonnie Heady were recommended for the death penalty by the jury. After just 15 minutes of deliberation by Judge Reeves, he agreed that death by execution fit the crime. Judge Reeves sentenced them both to be executed on December 18, 1953.

"I think the verdict fits the crime," Judge Reeves said. "It is the most coldblooded, brutal murder I have ever tried."

On December 18, 1953, Carl Hall and Bonnie Heady were set to die in the Missouri State Penitentiary in Jefferson City, Missouri. They were executed in the gas chamber. Less than three months after the kidnapping and murder of Bobby Greenlease, Carl Hall was pronounced dead at 12:12 A.M. and Bonnie Heady was pronounced dead just 20 seconds later. A case that gripped a nation was now officially closed.

Officially, only half of the $600,000 ransom was recovered by authorities. In the weeks following the execution, the next step for investigators was to locate the rest of the ransom money. It was determined that the two suitcases which contained the other half of the ransom money were never brought in to the police headquarters at the time of the arrest. While lacking any evidence, the state decided to pursue charges against Lieutenant Louis Ira Shoulders and Patrolman Elmer Dolan. Shoulders was found guilty on April 15, 1954 and subsequently sentenced to three years in federal prison. Elmer Dolan was tried on March 31, 1954. He was also found guilty and sentenced to two years in federal prison. Both men were convicted of perjury. Both men served their sentences, after which they returned to the St. Louis area. Lieutenant Louis Ira Shoulders passed away on May 12,

1962, never having the mistake reconciled. Elmer Dolan was officially pardoned by President Lyndon B. Johnson on July 21, 1965. The lack of evidence against these two men was overlooked, most likely due to circumstance and the relentless effort by the investigation teams to close the case.

The mysterious disappearance of the ransom money has been the source of many myths and conspiracies. To the day, the ransom money has never been recovered. Investigation into a number of conspiracies and theories has turned up no trace of evidence to support them. Perhaps to understand the crime, we must understand who Carl Hall and Bonnie Heady were. To go through with such a horrific act, these two people must have been psychopathic in nature. Their story is one of wonder and disgust, most easily understood by looking at the mental make-up of each and how their paths crossed.

Carl Hall enjoyed great wealth in his childhood. He was the son of a prestigious and wealthy St. Louis lawyer. Hall never had to do any real work for a living. His father passed in 1946, leaving a fortune of $200,000 to his son. Ironically, it was through a heavy drinking habit and drug addiction that he quickly squandered his entire fortune. This would mark the beginning of a downhill spiral for Carl Hall.

Carl Hall had wasted a massive fortune. His drug and alcohol addictions, however, still remained. Upon losing his money, he set out to robbing innocent taxi cab drivers. The epitome of a "five dollars at a time" living, his take was said to be $38 at the time of his capture. He was found guilty of robbery and served 16 months in a state prison, and was released on April 24, 1953. This was a mere five months before his participation in the kidnapping of Bobby Greenlease.

While serving his 16 month sentence at Missouri State Prison, Hall began planning the kidnapping and murder of six year old boy Bobby Greenlease. Bobby was the son of the wealthiest man in Kansas City, Missouri. Robert Cosgrove Greenlease Sr. had gained great wealth as a car dealer. He had gained the bulk of his fortune by introduction

General Motors vehicles to the Midwest. The 71 year old also had some family ties to Carl Hall.

As a child, Carl Hall attended military school at the same location as the adopted step-brother of Bobby Greenlease. While they were not friends nor did they even speak to each other, the knowledge of the family was bestowed upon Carl Hall. This would be one more thing to solidify the target of Hall and Heady.

On April 24, 1953, Carl Hall stepped out of prison. He was immediately embraced by a strange woman of whom he had never met before. This woman was Bonnie Brown Heady. She was 41 years old at the time and recently widowed. She was described as a plump, pale woman with a "porcine" face. The mysterious woman kissed Hall on the mouth and held him close. Only after her passionate kissing did she introduce herself to Hall.

Bonnie Brown Heady was a gun smuggler in the 1930's. It was in this line of work she met a bank robber named Dan Heady. Dan was a smuggler, bank robber, and overall low grade criminal of the late 1920's to the 1930's. Dan married Bonnie in 1935. It wasn't long until Dan was arrested for numerous crimes. He attempted to escape from prison to get to his young, red-headed wife Bonnie. He was gunned down by a group of sheriffs before he could fully escape. The story told by the sheriff who shot Dan Heady is a chilling insight into the kind of person that Bonnie was. Upon learning of the shooting and subsequent death of her husband, Bonnie was described as saying "well that's too bad" out of the side of a sly, almost happy grin. It was the lifestyle that Bonnie craved. She was attracted to criminals.

She had heard about who Carl Hall was and the life he lived through many ex-prisoners. She was intrigued. She was addicted to men like Carl Hall and Dan Heady. She was also addicted to heroin and was a heavy alcohol abuser, much like Hall. Upon introduction herself to Carl Hall, she took him to her home in St. Joseph, Missouri.

This would prove to be a grim foreshadowing of the events that would take place just over five months down the road.

It is well known that Bonnie Heady was a heavy drinker and heroin addict. Carl Hall was just as guilty as Bonnie was in this regard. They would spend nearly every waking day drinking themselves into a stupor together. When they weren't too drunk to function, they would near overdose on heroin with one another. This engulfed their lives in the 5 months after they had met. This was how they lived their life in Bonnie's home in St. Joseph, Missouri.

It was in the few sober times together that they began to plan the horrific crime they would soon carry out. While Hall had planned out most of the major details while in prison, Heady helped with the finer points of how they would work the ransom and different ways to obtain the ransom without being seen by authorities. When Carl Hall originally proposed she be an accomplice in his terrible plan, Bonnie famously remarked, "Why, that's better than sex!" She had fully agreed to participate.

The night before the duo carried out their kidnapping of Bobby Greenlease, the actions they took part in were a sickening omen. These events were focused on closely in court, as it proved that this was not only a pre-meditated kidnapping, but more importantly it was a pre-meditated murder.

It was pouring down rain the night of September 27, 1953. The couple, wearing heavy boots and rain coats, dug the shallow grave just outside the porch of Bonnie's St. Joseph home. This was the critical piece that allowed jurors to swiftly come to a death sentence after just an hour of deliberation.

The personality that Bonnie Heady and Carl Hall had was on full display in their ransom calls with the Greenleases. The following transcript is one of many, but shows a pattern of the mental games that Hall and Heady were playing with the Greenleases. In the transcript, Hall identifies himself as "M."

Mrs. Greenlease: Hello, this is Mrs. Greenlease.

M: M speaking.

Mrs. Greenlease: We have the money, but we must know that our son is alive and doing well. Could you at least give me that? Can't you give me something that will assure that?

M: That is a reasonable request. To be completely frank with you, this boy is driving us nuts. We couldn't possibly risk taking him to a phone.

Mrs. Greenlease: Well, I can only imagine. Can you do this then? Can you ask him two questions? Give me the answer to the two questions.

M: Well.

Mrs. Greenlease: If I had the answer to these two questions, I would trust and know that my son is alive and well.

M: All right.

Mrs. Greenlease: Ask him the name of our driver in Europe from this summer.

M: All right.

Mrs. Greenlease: The second question is what did you build with the monkey blocks in your playroom the last night you were home with us? If you can get those answers for me, I will feel better and relieved. You know that is the only thing that I want.

M: We have the boy. He is alive and well. Believe me. He is literally driving us crazy.

Mrs. Greenlease: Well I can imagine that. He is a very active little boy.

M: He has been driving us crazy.

Mrs. Greenlease: Could you please get those answers from him?

M: All right.

Bonnie and Carl delighted in these phone calls. The duo deliberately extended the negotiations. They would make several, as many as 15, brief phone calls. Each call would change the plans for the ransom in a way that would extend the process another day. The sadistic cat and mouse game that Hall and Heady were playing with the Greenleases was absolutely sickening. The process was also delayed, moreover, due to the drunkenness of the kidnappers.

Another crucial bit of information was the confession that Carl Hall made about the night he killed Bobby Greenlease. Hall said that he sent Bonnie to take a walk in the field so she didn't have to witness the killing, as well as to keep an eye out for witnesses. It was then that Hall tried to strangle the young boy to death. Even for a six year old boy, Hall said that Bobby was providing strong resistance to this. He was fighting for his life. This actual court record confession from Carl Hall is both chilling and heart breaking.

"I was prepared for that. I had the gun in my coat pocket," Hall said. "I pulled it out and shot once, trying to shoot him in the heart. I had no idea if I had hit him or not, for he was still alive. I shot him through the head on the second shot. I then took him out of the car and laid him there on the ground. I had a plastic bag that I put him in. I remember there being a lot of blood there. This farm, where the killing occurred, is about two miles south and two miles west of the state line."

"I then called on Bonnie to return to the car," Hall continued. "She walked back to the car and help me load the body in the trunk. We drove straight back to her home in St. Joseph. We had to wait until night fall to bury the body; we didn't want the neighbors to see our movements and get suspicious."

When Judge Reeves announced the sentencing, the courtroom broke out into a tearful applause. "I'd rather be dead than poor," Bonnie Heady famously sneered after the sentence announcement. Robert Cosgrove Greenlease Sr. sat through the court proceeding quietly throughout the trial. In the most famous words spoken after the trial from the Greenlease family, he famously said "It's too good for them, but it's the best the law provides."

On September 28, 1953, an innocent boy was taken from his school by sick criminals. An innocent boy was murdered that night by these same sadistic people. Throughout the entire ordeal, the quest for money was a central force in the murder of Bobby Greenlease. Another force, however, was the crazy mental states of a duo of heroin addicts and alcohol abusers who enjoyed the lifestyle. When all was said and done, the entire nation had been taken on an emotional rollercoaster that, sadly, didn't have the happy ending that everyone was hoping for. Instead, a six year old boy was murdered and, although justice was done, it still didn't seem to be enough. For people to deem it a possibility to take a child from school, it doesn't seem that there would ever be a punishment fitting enough to provide the end that was due. From a kidnapping that started on the morning of September 28, 1953, to the gas chamber on December 18, 1953, Bonnie Heady and Carl Hall remained twisted and miserable. All that the Greenlease family could do was wonder what Bobby could have matured into being.

CARMEN BUENO

Chile had been a hotbed for democratic unrest throughout most of the 20th century. It was into this time of unrest that on July 16, 1950, Carmen Cecilia Bueno Cifuentes was born in Santiago, Chile. But at the time of her birth, political violence had not yet reached its peak. Just as the life's journey of the infant Carmen Bueno had not yet been revealed, so too the human rights crimes, deaths and destruction that would result from the rule of General Pinochet had yet to be unveiled.

Few records exist of Bueno's parents and the conditions of her upbringing, but many of her later acquaintances remember her as a vibrant and passionate young woman. She first came to the attention of her fellow countrymen with the launch of her career as an actress. With her medium length dark hair cut into a sophisticated modern style and her dark eyes, her natural beauty soon caught the attention of filmmakers. After studying film at Pontificia Universidad Católica de Chile, the School of Art of Communication, her first major film appearance and the one that would solidify her career was La Tierra Prometida (The Promised Land). Bueno was 23 years old at the time and everyone believed that she had a promising career ahead of her.

The Promised Land

Directed by Miguel Littin, the film The Promised Land was released on September 11th, 1973. The tone of the film was out-and-out socialist in nature and strove to capture the lives of Chilean revolutionaries of the 1920s. Some believe that it was made in support of the Marxist ideals of Popularity Union, the political party led by Salvador Allende. It is described by IMDB as "an epic filmed ballad from Chile combining history and myth, allegory and revolution, spectacle and poetry."

Due to its content and openly socialist message, the film was released in Denmark, Sweden as it may have stirred unwanted attention in Chile. Though no immediate actions were taken against Bueno and her fellow thespians and film crew, which included Jorge Müller, the film may well have marked her as a political liability.

Jorge Müller

Born in 1947, Jorge Hernán Müller Silva was Bueno's senior by three years. The two shared a passion for filmmaking and worked together on two known projects. He had studies through the Film School of the University of Chile in Viña del Mar and rose to fame as a cinematographer and as the cameraman who shot the footage on the then-controversial three-part documentary film La Batalla de Chile (The Battle of Chile). He did the cinematography on many other films, including Descomedidos y chascones[1], Palomilla brava[2], and Socialist Realism[3] among others.

Some sources do not site the two filmmakers as being a couple, but those closest to them and who worked alongside them on films take it as a given that Bueno and Müller were romantically involved. This relationship may well have been spurred on by their shared love for film and their coinciding political views.

Aside from The Promised Land, Bueno and Müller were also part of the team responsible for creating the film A la Sombra del Sol. These were the only two films that they had a chance to work on together and were the only two films that Bueno acted in before her life was interrupted. Though Müller had gained more fame and notoriety because of the extent and novelty of his work, Bueno's contribution as both as actress, script writer and production assistant is undeniable.

The politics of the time

During the 1920s, the Chilean economy began to collapse. The country was plagued by one dictator after the other and experienced a period of intense political instability until the Radical Party won by popular vote in 1932 and remained in power for 20 years. 1952 saw the reappearance of former dictator Ibáñez del Campo, and in 1958, he was succeeded by Jorge Alessandri. During the 1964 elections,

---

1.   https://www.imdb.com/title/tt2943372/?ref_=nm_flmg_cin_6

2.   https://www.imdb.com/title/tt0070502/?ref_=nm_flmg_cin_7

3.   https://www.imdb.com/title/tt0070596/?ref_=nm_flmg_cin_8

Chilean rule fell to a Christian Democrat[4] by the name of Eduardo Frei Montalva[5], who made many radical changes to the country, including the unionisation of farm labourers. His dream for a reformed Chile would not be realised before he was ousted by Senator Salvador Allende in 1970.

All of these political changes, though for the most part democratic in their execution, indicated that the general population was divided as to what type of government should lead Chile forward. Moving between far right and far left leaders, this would prove to be a foreshadowing of the political turmoil that would eventually erupt and engulf the country.

Through her participation in politically imbued films, it is clear that Bueno already had established political ideas counter to what some Chileans deemed as acceptable political views.

General Pinochet's coup

Augusto José Ramón Pinochet Ugarte was a ruthless dictator who took control of Chile by means of military force during his coup d'état on September 11th, 1973. For the next 17 years, he would rule the country with an iron fist, committing multiple crimes against humanity and suppressing freedom of expression on many levels, especially in the arts and film industries. After Salvador Allende of the socialist Popular Unity party won the 1973 presidential elections, the country was divided and there was talk of the possible outbreak of a civil war. Ironically, it had been Allende himself who, less than a month before, had promoted Pinochet to the Chilean national army's Commander-in-Chief.

The idea that the military coup was backed by the United States government is generally accepted and discussed by various historians and scholars. It put Pinochet in control of almost every aspect of life in Chile to which any criticism was met with detainment, torture or

---

4.   https://en.wikipedia.org/wiki/Christian_Democrat_Party_of_Chile

5.   https://en.wikipedia.org/wiki/Eduardo_Frei_Montalva

execution. Any supporters of the previous democratically elected government were closely scrutinized along with any groups or individuals with leftist ideas. Trade unions were banned and the privatisation of many state-owned businesses. These actions stabilised Chile's economy but also caused extensive economic differences between the working class, who had been Marxist supporters, and the upper and middle classes.

Though some good came from Pinochet's takeover, what followed was for the most part a reign of terror that still remains as a sore point in the country's history. The violence of the coup saw many die in the fight for freedom and a fair democratically elected government, but not nearly as many as would loose their lives in the years to come.

Pinochet's time as supreme leader came to an end in 1990 when he was succeeded by Patricio Aylwin. This change in leadership was made possible by the 1988 plebiscite during which 56% of voters were against the continued rule by Pinochet. He effectively stepped down on March 11th, 1990 but remained as the Commander-in-Chief of the Chilean Army for another 8 years. On October 10th, 1998 he was arrested while on a visit to London and charged with hundreds of crimes, including human rights violations, involvement in arms deals, tax fraud and embezzlement. Ill health got him back to Chile without being persecuted but in 2004 he was placed under house arrest by Judge Juan Guzmán Tapia[6]. House arrest would unfortunately be the worst sentence he served before his death on December 10th, 2006. Most of his crimes remained unaccounted for, including the near 30 million USD he had embezzled over the years.

The Battle of Chile

An enticing piece of documentary filmmaking, The Battle of Chile starts off with footage of the bombing of a Chilean parliamentary building. The bombing occurred merely a few months after General

---

6.   https://en.wikipedia.org/wiki/Juan_Guzm%252525C3%252525A1n_Tapia

Pinochet's military takeover of the country. Pauline Kael, a writer for the New Yorker, said of the film: "We actually see a country cracking open." Much of the film's footage is of a brave interviewer asking civilians and ordinary people in the street about their political opinions, with Müller operating the camera in pursuit. It was an innovative way of documentary filmmaking and captures the essence of the time in a way that is not commonly seen.

The film was divided into three parts; La insurrección de la burguesía (The Insurrection of the Bourgeoisie), El golpe de estado (The Government Coup), and El poder popular (The Popular Power). The films were released in 1975, 1976, and 1979 respectively. In the introductory scene of the first film, an in memoria note is dedicated to Jorge Müller.

In an article for Archive by Claudia Dreifus, Patricio Guzman, the director and mastermind behind the film, reported "I was always asking exiles, 'This worker at that factory, what has happened to him?' The people in 'The Battle of Chile' were well known. So, there was reason to worry." Guzman had gone into exile in fear of his life and for political reasons after Bueno, Müller and others began disappearing.

Political involvement and the MIR

Bueno and Müller were both members of the MIR, Movimiento de Izquierda Revolucionaria or The Movement of the Revolutionary Left. It is unclear when they became affiliated with the group, but like many other young Chileans, they believed that it was the best way to rally against the political atrocities that were occurring in the country on a near-daily base.

The group was founded in 1965 and by 1973 numbered in the thousands, some estimates regarding the official count as over 10 000 strong. No exact number is known due to some members preferring to keep their identities secret. Bueno and Müller, on the other hand, were known to be members of the organisation. The MIR consisted mainly of students, were closely associated with the People's Democratic

Movement and workers' unions, and upheld a Marxist–Leninist[7] variety of communist[8] ideology.

The MIR was actively militant in nature and played a part in the Resistance against General Pinochet's coup d'état. Some of the group's members lost their lives in the fighting. After Pinochet's successful military coup, the MIR leader, Miguel Enríquez Espinosa[9], was assassinated by members of the DINA (Dirección de Inteligencia Nacional or the National Intelligence Directorate)in 1974. The MIR remained active throughout the 1980s and into the 1990s despite attempts to eradicate the group by any means.

A la Sombra del Sol

The last film Carmen Bueno and Jorge Müller ever had the chance to work on was A la Sombra del Sol (In the Shadow of the Sun). Directed by Silvio Caiozzi and Pablo Perelman, it is based on true events and tells the story of two prison escapees who cross the Atacama Desert on their way to Bolivia. They come across the town of Caspana, where they are welcomed by locals, but after the fugitives are accused of raping two female pastors, they are sentenced to death by a community tribunal.

Bueno starred in the film and also fulfilled the role of script writer and other smaller film industry related tasks. Müller was part of the camera crew. Though the film caused some hype upon its release on November 28th, 1974, not all of the attention was positive. Pinochet's regime was one of suppression and artists in particular were targeted if their creative expressions did not sit right with the new regime.

In many ways, the work done by Carmen Bueno, Jorge Müller and many of their contemporaries was at the forefront of filmmaking in Chile. They were the avantgarde of national cinema and did not shy

---

7.   https://en.wikipedia.org/wiki/Marxism%252525E2%25252580%25252593Leninism

8.   https://en.wikipedia.org/wiki/Communism

9.   https://en.wikipedia.org/wiki/Miguel_Enr%252525C3%252525ADquez_Espinosa

away from the threats that they were constantly subjected to. Many of them paid for their love for art with their lives, but their legacy remains.

Disappearance

It was a day after the official premier of A la Sombra del Sol at around 9:30pm on Novemeber 29th, 1974 when Bueno and Müller were kidnapped. They had attended the first showing of the film together the previous evening and were on their way to Müller's house after which they intended to stop by Chile Films where they both worked. They would never reach their destinations, though, as they were taken in full public view on Bilbao street. The couple were thrown into a van by men dressed as civilians but who were clearly members of DINA.

The couple were detained at the infamous Villa Grimaldi, where they were reportedly interrogated and tortured. A week or so later, they allegedly disappeared and remain missing to this day. It has been presumed that like many others, they disappeared while being transported from Cuatro Alamos, a stop off prison and torture detention camp between Villa Grimaldi and Tres Alamos. At Cuatro Alamos, other detained claimed to have seen the pair, but what happened to them after being loaded into a transport van is unknown. No one has come forth to make any further statements regarding the fate that befell the two filmmakers. Indications are not good, however, since almost no survivors ever escaped Villa Grimaldi.

In the Jump Cut article, no. 8, 1975, p. 25, it was reported that "among the most recent victims of Chile's military junta are Carmen Bueno... and Jorge Muller." The article, though a few months late, further reported that "On November 29, 1974, while working on a documentary for the Peace Committee of the Chilean Churches, Carmen and Jorge were forced into a car and abducted by agents of the infamous Dirección Nacional de Inteligencia (DINA), an agency modeled after the Nazi Gestapo. Little been available as to either their whereabouts or their physical condition and their families and friends have been unable to contact them."

56 former DINA members all received prison sentences in 2015 for the horrors they meted out at Villa Grimaldi. One of the crimes they were found guilty of was the torture of Carmen Bueno and Jorge Müller, but not one of them could say what happened to the couple after their ordeal.

The prison-like building on Avenida José Arrieta 8200, in the Peñalolén sector, with its painted brick front and square guard tower, has since been made into a museum and memorial for all those who entered through its doors and never come out again. Photos of those fearless individual who stood against the inhuman and criminal acts of Chile's dictator can be seen on display just within the villa's border walls. Carmen Bueno's photo, along with that of Jorge Müller's, is among them.

It was reported by in the National Commission on Political Imprisonment and Torture's Valech Report and also by Commission of Truth and Reconciliation's Rettig Report that approximately 30 000 Chileans were victims of torture and other human rights violations under the directions of General Pinochet's brutal regime. Some reports put the number of individuals who were arrested, interrogatedor and tortured as high as 80 000. Of these victims, there is definitive proof that just over 2200 of them were executed. Many thousands remain missing even today, with Carmen Bueno and Jorge Müller among them.

In memoria

To this day, Carmen Bueno's name appears alongside that of many others who disappeared under suspicious circumstances under Pinochet's rule and who have not been found. Almost all the disappearances in Chile during this time have been attributed to DINA and were political in nature.

Although she has been missing for over 43 years, having disappeared at the age of only 24, Carmen Bueno not been forgotten. Her sister, Maria Olimpia Bueno has written a poem about her titled "Sister Girl" as part of a request for any information on her whereabouts. A quote from the poem, which was originally written in Spanish, contains a glimpse of Bueno's patriotism and her dedication to the fight against Pinochet's dictatorship:

"Your love for life and for man will lead you to fight for justice alongside your people."

Another poem by María Elena Blanco titled "Mutilated Letters" is a tribute to the lives of both Bueno and Müller.

The book *Tapestries of Hope, Threads of Love: The Arpillera Movement in Chile* by Marjorie Agosín[10] was first published on July 1st, 1996 by Rowman and Littlefield Publishers. It describes the lives and struggles of ordinary Chilean women between 1973 and 1989 who made arpilerras as a form of silent protest. Arpilerras were scraps of cloth onto which was handstitched memorials to all those who disappeared during Pinochet's rule of brutality. None of the missing persons depicted by their relatives on the arpilerras has ever been found alive. Müller's mother contributed to the book, speaking out about her son and Bueno. The author and editor of the book is herself a political exile from Chile and has written

---

10. https://www.goodreads.com/author/show/ 222743.Marjorie_Agos_n

biographies and critical essays on social issues, such as *Secrets in the Sand: The Young Women of Juarez*[11] and *Women, Gender and Human Rights: A Global Perspective*. She has also written works of poetry relating to Latin American culture and history, including *I Lived on Butterfly Hill*. The book was translated to English by Celeste Kostopulos-Cooperman[12] and a second edition was printed in October, 2007.

The International Human Rights Project runs the website memoriaviva.com (Living Memory). The goal of the site is described as a 'digital file of the Violations of Human Rights by the Military Dictatorship in Chile (1973-1990)' and intends to keep the memories of individuals such as Carmen Bueno and Jorge Müller alive.

Many organisations and exist around the world that are dedicated to find the truth behind the Chilean disappearances. These groups exist as a continued effort to locate individuals who went missing during the time of Pinochet's human rights violations.

The end to Carmen Bueno's tragic story may never be discovered. She will be remembered for the contributions she made to Chilean national cinema and the risks she took to vocalise and show the country as it was during its most recent time of political unrest. Her memory is a constant reminder of Chile's cruel and violent history and should serve as a beacon in the way forward so that the mistakes of the past may never be repeated.

---

11. *https://www.goodreads.com/book/show/*
    178174.Secrets_in_the_Sand
12. https://www.goodreads.com/author/show/
    181663.Celeste_Kostopulos_Cooperman